# The Grimoire of Arundell: Conjuring Angels, Demons, Fairies, and the Dead

# The Grimoire of Arundell: Conjuring Angels, Demons, Fairies, and the Dead
## by
## Arundell Overman

ISBN(9798355381240)

# Table of Contents

The magic circle page 10
Evocation (To call forth any spirit) page 11
                              List of spirits

## Demons

Agaliarept page 14
Agares page 16
Aglasis page 17
Aim page 18
Alloces page 19
Amdusias page 20
Amy page 21
Andras page 22
Andrealphus page 23
Andromalius page 24
Amon page 25
Asmodeus page 26
Astaroth page 28
Azazel page 30
Bael page 31
Balam page 32
Barbatos page 33
Bathin page 34
Bechard page 35
Beleth page 37
Belial page 39
Belzebub page 40
Berith page 41
Bifrons page 42
Botis page 43
Brulefer page 44
Bucon page 46
Buer page 48

Bune page 49
Camio page 50
Cemejes page 51
Claunech page 52
Clisthert page 53
Crocell page 55
Dantalion page 56
Decarabia page 57
Egyn page 58
Elelogap page 60
Eligos page 62
Fleurety page 63
Focalor page 65
Foras page 66
Forneus page 67
Frimost page 68
Frucissiere page 70
Frutimiere page 72
Furcas page 74
Furfur page 75
Gaap page 76
Glasya-Labolas page 77
Gremory page 78
Guland page 79
Gusion page 81
Haagenti page 82
Hael page 83
Halphus page 85
Haristum page 86
Haures page 88
Heramael page 89
Hicpacth page 91
Huictigaras page 93
Humots page 95
Ipos page 97

Khil page 98
Klepoth page 100
Leraje page 102
Leviathan page 103
Lilith page 104
Lucifer page 105
Lucifuge Rofocale page 107
Malphas page 108
Marax page 109
Marbas page 110
Marchosias page 111
Mersilde page 112
Minoson page 114
Morail page 115
Murmur page 117
Musisin page 118
Naberius page 120
Nebiros page 121
Oriax page 123
Oriens page 124
Orobas page 126
Ose page 127
Paimon page 128
Pentagnony page 130
Phenex page 132
Proculo page 133
Pruflas page 135
Purson page 137
Raum page 138
Ronove page 139
Sabnock page 140
Sallos page 141
Samigina page 142
Sargatanas page 143
Satanachia page 145

Scirlin page 146
Seere page 148
Segal page 149
Sergulath page 151
Serguthy page 153
Shax page 155
Sidragosam page 156
Sirchade page 158
Sitri page 160
Stolas page 161
Surgat page 162
Sustugriel page 164
Syrach page 166
Trimasael page 168
Uvall page 170
Valak page 171
Valefor page 172
Vapula page 173
Vassago page 174
Vepar page 175
Vine page 176
Zagan page 177
Zepar page 178

# Fairies

Oberon page 180
Mycob page 180
Lilia page 181
Rostilia page 181
Foca page 181
Fola page 181
Africa page 182
Julia page 182
Venulla page 182
Sibylia page 183

Milia page 183
Achilia page 183
Michel page 185
Chicam page 185
Burfee page 185

# The Dead

V.B. page 186

# Angels

Michael page 188
Gabriel page 188
Samael page 189
Raphael page 189
Sachiel page 190
Anael page 190
Cassiel page 190
Metatron page 191

Notes on the work 192
The creation of the universal conjuring circle 197

## EVOCATION (To call forth any spirit)

1. Enter into the magic circle after drawing it on the ground or on the back of a rug or carpet, along with the triangle. Raise the magic wand, and say: "MY NAME IS............... I HAVE PURIFIED MY MIND AND BODY. I HAVE COMPLETED MY WORK WITHIN THE WORLD. THUS, MAY I ENTER INTO THE TEMPLE OF THE INFINITE AND BEHOLD THE SERPENT BITING ITS OWN TAIL. THIS IS THE PRAYER OF THE SNAKE."

2. Recite the bornless invocation. Raise the wand and say: "THEE I INVOKE THE BORNLESS ONE! THEE THAT DIDST CREATE THE EARTH AND THE HEAVENS! THEE THAT DIDST CREATE THE DARKNESS AND THE LIGHT!" "THOU DIDST MAKE THE FEMALE AND THE MALE! THOU DIDST PRODUCE THE SEED AND THE FRUIT! THOU DIDST FORM MEN AND WOMEN TO LOVE ONE ANOTHER AND TO HATE ONE ANOTHER!"

"I INVOKE THEE, THE TERRIBLE AND INVISIBLE GOD WHO DWELLEST IN THE VOID PLACE OF THE SPIRIT! AROGOGORO BRAO, SOTHU, MODORIO, PHALARTHAO, DOO, APE, THE BORNLESS ONE! HEAR ME!" "I AM HE! (OR SHE IF THE ONE CALLING THE SPIRITS IS A WOMAN) THE BORNLESS SPIRIT, HAVING SIGHT IN THE FEET, STRONG AND THE IMMORTAL FIRE! I AM HE, THE TRUTH! I AM HE, THE GRACE OF THE WORLD! THE HEART GIRT WITH A SERPENT IS MY NAME!"

"COME THOU FORTH AND FOLLOW ME, AND MAKE ALL SPIRITS SUBJECT UNTO ME, SO THAT EVERY SPIRIT OF THE FIRNAMENT AND OF THE ETHER, UPON THE EARTH AND UNDER THE EARTH, ON DRY LAND AND IN THE WATER, OF WHIRLING AIR AND OF RUSHING FIRE, AND EVERY SPELL AND SCOURGE OF GOD MAY BE OBEDIENT UNTO ME!"

3. Now raise the wand and conjure the spirit with these words: "I EVOKE AND CONJURE THEE O THOU SPIRIT...............AND BEING ARMED WITH POWER FROM THE SUPREME MAJESTY, I DO STRONGLY COMMAND THEE."
"COME! APPEAR BEFORE THIS CIRCLE, AND WITHIN THAT TRIANGLE, NOW AND WITHOUT DELAY, MANIFESTING THAT WHICH I SHALL DESIRE, FOR THOU ART CONJURED BY THE NAME OF THE LIVING AND TRUE GOD HELIOREN!"

"I CONJURE THEE BY THE NAME NO CREATURE IS ABLE TO RESIST, THE MIGHTY TETRAGRAMMATON, AH-MAH-SHAH-OH, THE POWER THAT MAKES THE WIND BLOW, THE FIRE BURN, THE SEA ROLL BACK, THE EARTH MOVE, AND ALL THE HOST OF HEAVEN, EARTH, AND HELL TO TREMBLE!"

4. When the spirit appears say to it: "I WELCOME THEE SPIRIT………… I THANK THEE FOR HEEDING MY SUMMONS. BY THE POWER OF GOD, I COMMAND THEE TO REMAIN BEFORE THIS CIRCLE AND WITHIN THAT TRIANGLE, GIVING ME TRUE ANSWERS AND FAITHFUL SERVICE UNTIL I SHALL LICENSE THEE TO DEPART."

5. Offer incense as a gift to the spirit. (Or Everclear and a tiny amount of your own blood, mixed together and set on fire)

6. Converse with the spirit. (Or perform other works of magic such as Invisibility, Transformation, The Sabbath, or Talismans)

7. When done speaking with the spirit say: "OH THOU SPIRIT…………… I NOW LICENSE THEE TO DEPART UNTO THY PROPER PLACE. MAY THE PEACE OF GOD EVER CONTINUE BETWEEN THEE AND ME. DEPART, DEPART, DEPART I SAY AND BE GONE!"

# Demons

**Agaliarept**

Agalierept and Tarchimache (Lucifuge Rofocale) are the rulers of Elelogap, who in turn governs matters connected with water. - Grimorium Verum

Agaliarept, who has the power to discover the most hidden secrets, in all the Courts and Governments of the world, he reveals the greatest mysteries. He commands the second legion of spirits, he has under him Buer, Gusoan and Botis. - The Grand Grimoire.

Notes: Sigil from The Grand Grimoire, image created by my art team.

**Agares**

A Duke called Agreas, or Agares. He is under the Power of the East, and cometh up in the form of an old fair Man, riding upon a Crocodile, carrying a Goshawk upon his fist, and yet mild in appearance. He maketh them to run that stand still, and bringeth back runaways. He teaches all Languages or Tongues presently. He hath power also to destroy Dignities both Spiritual and Temporal, and causeth Earthquakes. He was of the Order of Virtues. He hath under his government 31 Legions of Spirits. And this is his Seal or Character which thou shalt wear as a Lamen before thee. -Lesser Key of Solomon.

Notes: Image from the Dictionnaire Infernal, sigil from the Lesser Key.

**Aglasis**

Aglasis, who can carry anyone or anything anywhere in the world. - Grimorium Verum. Notes: Sigil created by the author, image by the art team.

**Aim**

Aim. He is a Great Strong Duke. He appeareth in the form of a very handsome Man in body, but with three Heads; the first, like a Serpent, the second like a Man having two Stars on his Forehead, the third like a Calf. He rideth on a Viper, carrying a Firebrand in his Hand, wherewith he setteth cities, castles, and great Places, on fire. He maketh thee witty in all manner of ways, and giveth true answers unto private matters. He governeth 26 Legions of Inferior Spirits; and his Seal is this, which wear thou as aforesaid, etc. -Lesser Key of Solomon

Notes: Image from the Dictionnaire Infernal, sigil from the Lesser Key of Solomon.

**Alloces**

Alloces, or Alocas. He is a Duke, Great, Mighty, and Strong, appearing in the Form of a Soldier riding upon a Great Horse. His Face is like that of a Lion, very Red, and having Flaming Eyes. His Speech is hoarse and very big. His Office is to teach the Art of Astronomy, and all the Liberal Sciences. He bringeth unto thee Good Familiars; also he ruleth over 36 Legions of Spirits. His Seal is this, which, etc. -Lesser Key of Solomon

Notes: Image from the Dictionnaire Infernal, sigil from the Lesser Key of Solomon.

**Amdusias**

Amdusias, or Amdukias. He is a Duke Great and Strong, appearing at first like a Unicorn, but at the request of the Exorcist he standeth before him in Human Shape, causing Trumpets, and all manner of Musical Instruments to be heard, but not soon or immediately. Also, he can cause Trees to bend and incline according to the Exorcist's Will. He giveth Excellent Familiars. He governeth 29 Legions of Spirits. And his Seal is this, etc. -Lesser Key of Solomon

Notes: Image from the Dictionnaire Infernal, sigil from the Lesser Key of Solomon.

**Amy**

Amy, or Avnas. He is a Great President, and appeareth at first in the Form of a Flaming Fire; but after a while he putteth on the Shape of a Man. His office is to make one Wonderful Knowing in Astrology and all the Liberal Sciences. He giveth Good Familiars and can bewray Treasure that is kept by Spirits. He governeth 36 Legions of Spirits, and his Seal is this, etc. -Lesser Key of Solomon

Notes: Image by my art team, sigil from the Lesser Key of Solomon.

**Andras**

Andras. He is a Great Marquis, appearing in the Form of an Angel with a Head like a Black Night Raven, riding upon a strong Black Wolf, and having a Sharp and Bright Sword flourished aloft in his hand. His Office is to sow Discords. If the Exorcist have not a care, he will slay both him and his fellows. He governeth 30 Legions of Spirits, and this is his Seal, etc. -Lesser Key of Solomon

Notes: Image from the Dictionnaire Infernal, sigil from the Lesser Key of Solomon.

**Andrealphus**

Andrealphus. He is a Mighty Marquis, appearing at first in the form of a Peacock, with great Noises. But after a time he putteth on Human shape. He can teach Geometry perfectly. He maketh Men very subtle therein; and in all Things pertaining unto Mensuration or Astronomy. He can transform a Man into the Likeness of a Bird. He governeth 30 Legions of Infernal Spirits, and his Seal is this, etc. -Lesser Key of Solomon

Notes. Public domain image of a peacock, sigil from the Lesser Key of Solomon.

**Andromalius**

Andromalius. He is an Earl, Great and Mighty, appearing in the Form of a Man holding a Great Serpent in his Hand. His Office is to bring back both a Thief, and the Goods which be stolen; and to discover all Wickedness, and Underhand Dealing; and to punish all Thieves and other Wicked People; and also to discover Treasures that be Hid. He ruleth over 36 Legions of Spirits. His Seal is this, the which wear thou as aforesaid, etc. -Lesser Key of Solomon.

Notes: Sigil from the Lesser Key, image drawn by my art team.

**Amon**

Amon. He is a Marquis great in power, and most stern. He appeareth like a Wolf with a Serpent's tail, vomiting out of his mouth flames of fire; but at the command of the Magician he putteth on the shape of a Man with Dog's teeth beset in a head like a Raven; or else like a Man with a Raven's head (simply). He telleth all things Past and to Come. He procureth feuds and reconcileth controversies between friends. He governeth 40 Legions of Spirits. His Seal is this which is to be worn as aforesaid, etc. -Lesser Key of Solomon

Notes: Image from the Dictionnaire Infernal, sigil from the Lesser Key of Solomon.

## Asmodeus

Asmoday, or Asmodai. He is a Great King, Strong, and Powerful. He appeareth with Three Heads, whereof the first is like a Bull, the second like a Man, and the third like a Ram; he hath also the tail of a Serpent, and from his mouth issue Flames of Fire. His Feet are webbed like those of a Goose. He sitteth upon an Infernal Dragon, and beareth in his hand a Lance with a Banner. He is first and choicest under the Power of AMAYMON, he goeth before all other. When the Exorcist hath a mind to call him, let it be abroad, and let him stand on his feet all the time of action, with his Cap or Head-dress off; for if it be on, AMAYMON will deceive him and call all his actions to be bewrayed. But as soon as the Exorcist seeth Asmoday in the shape aforesaid, he shall call him by his Name, saying: "Art thou Asmoday?" and he will not deny it, and by-and-by he will bow down unto the ground. He giveth the Ring of Virtues; he teacheth the Arts of Arithmetic, Astronomy, Geometry, and all handicrafts absolutely. He giveth true and full answers unto thy demands. He maketh one Invincible. He showeth the place where Treasures lie, and guardeth it. He, amongst the Legions of AMAYMON governeth 72 Legions of Spirits Inferior. His Seal is this which thou must wear as a Lamen upon thy breast, etc. -Lesser Key of Solomon

Notes: Image from the Dictionnaire Infernal, sigil from the Lesser Key of Solomon.

**Astaroth**

Astaroth. He is a Mighty, Strong Duke, and appeareth in the Form of an hurtful Angel riding on an Infernal Beast like a Dragon, and carrying in his right hand a Viper. Thou must in no wise let him approach too near unto thee, lest he do thee damage by his Noisome Breath. Wherefore the Magician must hold the Magical Ring near his face, and that will defend him. He giveth true answers of things Past, Present, and to Come, and can discover all Secrets. He will declare wittingly how the Spirits fell, if desired, and the reason of his own fall. He can make men wonderfully knowing in all Liberal Sciences. He ruleth 40 Legions of Spirits. His Seal is this, which wear thou as a Lamen before thee, or else he will not appear nor yet obey thee, etc. -Lesser Key of Solomon

Notes: The demon Astaroth is also the Canaanite goddess Astarte. This image of the demon was created by my art team. The sigils are from the Lesser Key of Solomon, Grand Grimoire, and Grimoire of Armadel.

**Azazel**

Azazel. He is the leader of the Shedim, or hairy goat demons of the desert. He was the first fallen angel. He taught the secrets of warfare to men and the knowledge of seduction through cosmetics and jewelry to women. He is known as the father of witches and sorcery and can open the Sabbath, a gathering of witches. He can give you any familiar spirit or teach you how to cast any spell. He rules 666 legions.

Notes: Image of Azazel from the Dictionnaire Infernal, sigil by the author.

## Bael

A King ruling in the East, called Bael. He maketh thee to go Invisible. He ruleth over 66 Legions of Infernal Spirits. He appeareth in divers shapes, sometimes like a Cat, sometimes like a Toad, and sometimes like a Man, and sometimes all these forms at once. He speaketh hoarsely. This is his character which is used to be worn as a Lamen before him who calleth him forth, or else he will not do thee homage. - Lesser Key of Solomon

Notes: (also gives wisdom) Image from the Dictionnaire Infernal, sigil from the Lesser Key of Solomon. Bael is the Canaanite god Baal Hadad.

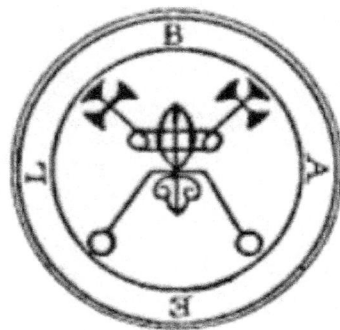

**Balam**

Balam or Balaam. He is a Terrible, Great, and Powerful King. He appeareth with three Heads: the first is like that of a Bull; the second is like that of a Man; the third is like that of a Ram. He hath the Tail of a Serpent, and Flaming Eyes. He rideth upon a furious Bear, and carrieth a Goshawk upon his Fist. He speaketh with a hoarse Voice, giving True Answers of Things Past, Present, and to Come. He maketh men to go Invisible, and also to be Witty. He governeth 40 Legions of Spirits. His Seal is this, etc. -Lesser Key of Solomon

Notes: Image from the Dictionnaire Infernal, sigil from the Lesser Key of Solomon.

**Barbatos**

Barbatos. He is a Great Duke, and appeareth when the Sun is in Sagittary, with four noble Kings and their companies of great troops. He giveth understanding of the singing of Birds, and of the Voices of other creatures, such as the barking of Dogs. He breaketh the Hidden Treasures open that have been laid by the Enchantments of Magicians. He is of the Order of Virtues, of which some part he retaineth still; and he knoweth all things Past, and to Come, and conciliateth Friends and those that be in Power. He ruleth over 30 Legions of Spirits. His Seal of Obedience is this, the which wear before thee as aforesaid. -Lesser Key of Solomon

Notes: Image from the Dictionnaire Infernal, sigil from the Lesser Key of Solomon.

**Bathin**

   Bathin. He is a Mighty and Strong Duke, and appeareth like a Strong Man with the tail of a Serpent, sitting upon a Pale-coloured Horse. He knoweth the Virtues of Herbs and Precious Stones, and can transport men suddenly from one country to another. He ruleth over 30 Legions of Spirits. His Seal is this which is to be worn as aforesaid. -Lesser Key of Solomon

Notes: Image by my art team, sigils from the Lesser Key of Solomon.

# Bechard

Bechard is a demon described in the Keys of Solomon as having power over winds and storms. He causes hail, storms, and rain, by means of a malefic curse that he composes with stewed toads and other drugs. - Dictionnaire Infernal, 1863

Notes: The illustration of a toad represents Bechard. The grimoire of Honorius says that he should be invoked on a Friday and given a nut. Sigils from the Grimorium Verum and Secrets of Solomon. Image of the demon drawn by my art team.

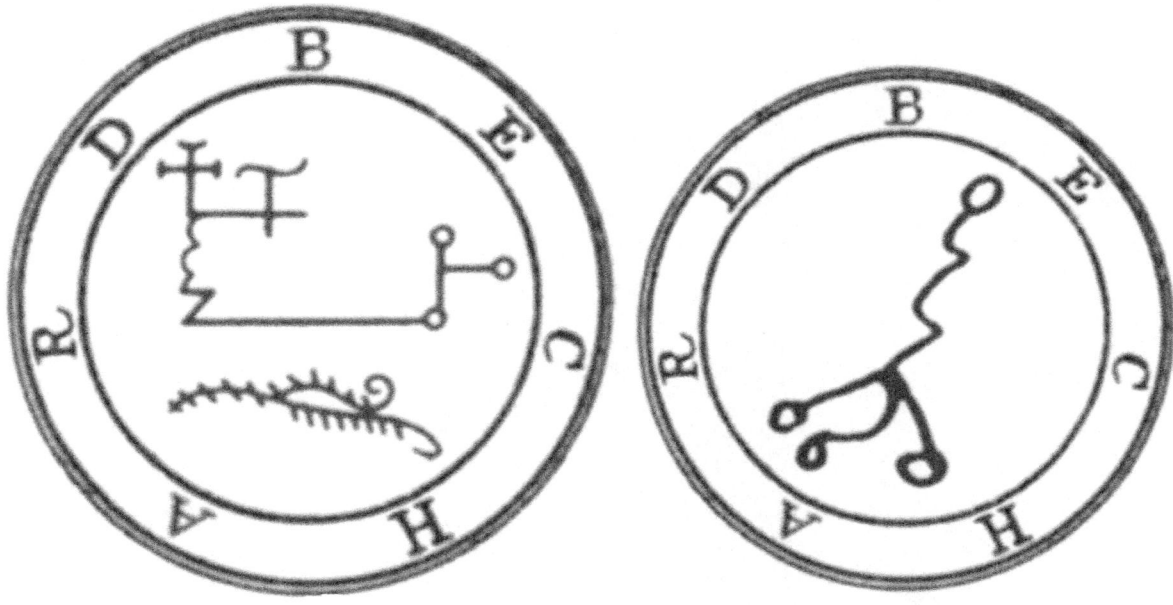

## Beleth

Beleth (or Bileth, or Bilet). He is a mighty King and terrible. He rideth on a pale horse with trumpets and other kinds of musical instruments playing before him. He is very furious at his first appearance, that is, while the Exorcist layeth his courage; for to do this he must hold a Hazel Wand in his hand, striking it out towards the South and East Quarters, make a triangle, Δ, without the Circle, and then command him into it by the Bonds and Charges of Spirits as hereafter followeth. And if he doth not enter into the triangle, Δ, at your threats, rehearse the Bonds and Charms before him, and then he will yield Obedience and come into it, and do what he is commanded by the Exorcist. Yet he must receive him courteously because he is a Great King, and do homage unto him, as the Kings and Princes do that attend upon him. And thou must have always a Silver Ring on the middle finger of the left hand held against thy face, as they do yet before AMAYMON. This Great King Beleth causeth all the love that may be, both of Men and of Women, until the Master Exorcist hath had his desire fulfilled. He is of the Order of Powers, and he governeth 85 Legions of Spirits. His Noble Seal is this, which is to be worn before thee at working. -Lesser Key of Solomon

Notes: Image from the Dictionnaire Infernal. The image shows one of the lesser demons under the command of Beleth, and the Dictionnaire Infernal states that cats who blow the horn go before the demon to announce his presence. Sigils from the Lesser Key of Solomon. Here is where we see the use of a Hazel wand which is found in many grimoires such as the Lesser Key of Solomon, Grand Grimoire, Black Dragon, and Discoverie of Witchcraft. The triangle being already made, the student should arm him or herself with a wand of Hazel...

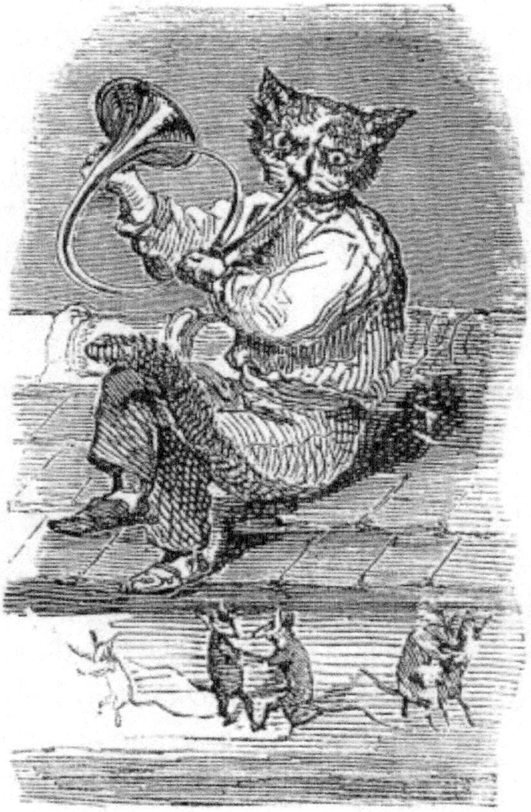

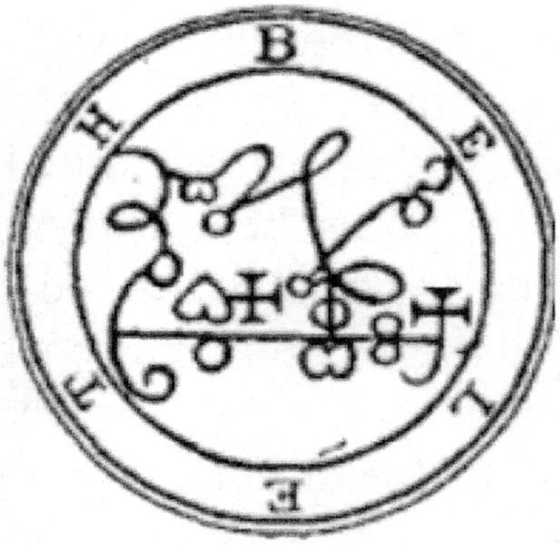

B
E
L
E
T
H

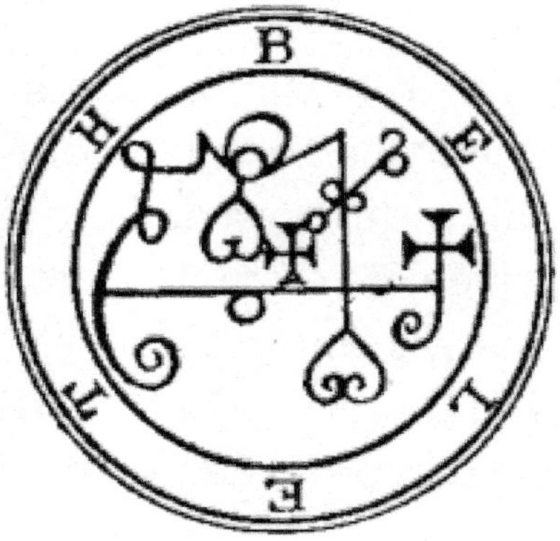

B
E
L
E
T
H

**Belial**

Belial. He is a Mighty and a Powerful King, and was created next after LUCIFER. He appeareth in the Form of Two Beautiful Angels sitting in a Chariot of Fire. He speaketh with a Comely Voice, and declareth that he fell first from among the worthier sort, that were before Michael, and other Heavenly Angels. His Office is to distribute Presentations and Senatorships, etc., and to cause favour of Friends and of Foes. He giveth excellent Familiars, and governeth 50 Legions of Spirits. Note well that this King Belial must have Offerings, Sacrifices and Gifts presented unto him by the Exorcist, or else he will not give True Answers unto his Demands. But then he tarrieth not one hour in the Truth, unless he be constrained by Divine Power. And his Seal is this, which is to be worn as aforesaid, etc. -Lesser Key of Solomon. Notes: Sigil from the Lesser Key of Solomon, image of the demon from "The Magus" by Francis Barett.

## Belzebuth

Belzebuth. He appears in the form of a giant fly or bee, also he may appear in the form of a monstrous goat or calf. He has the power to cause hypnotic illusions, seeming to transform men into beasts, and beasts into men. He is the founder of the order of the fly. He can teach the magician how to cast curses. He rules 500 legions.

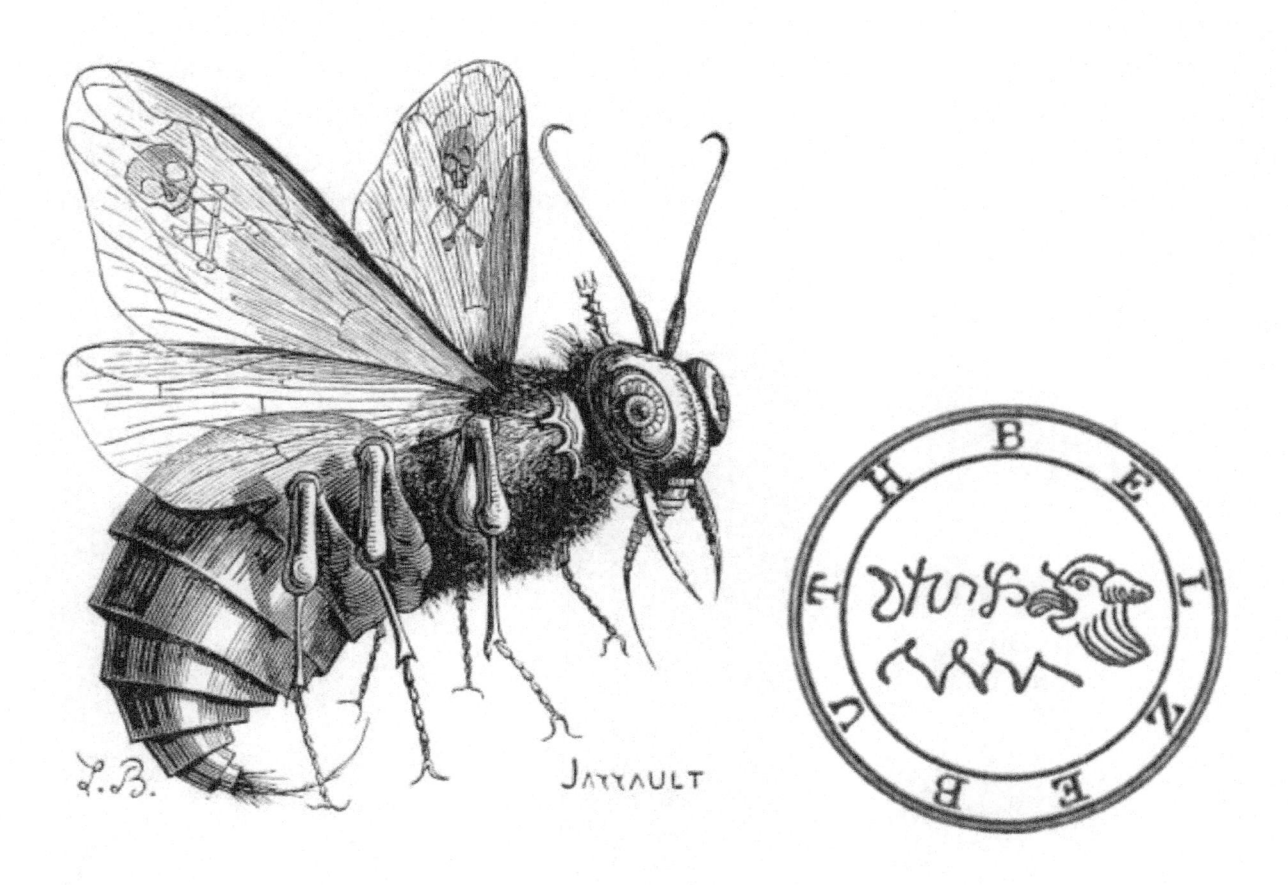

**Berith**

Berith. He is a Mighty, Great, and Terrible Duke. He hath two other Names given unto him by men of later times, viz: BEALE, or BEAL, and BOFRY or BOLFRY. He appeareth in the Form of a Soldier with Red Clothing, riding upon a Red Horse, and having a Crown of Gold upon his head. He giveth true answers, Past, Present, and to Come. Thou must make use of a Ring in calling him forth, as is before spoken of regarding Beleth. He can turn all metals into Gold. He can give Dignities, and can confirm them unto Man. He speaketh with a very clear and subtle Voice. He is a Great Liar, and not to be trusted unto. He governeth 26 Legions of Spirits. His Seal is this, etc. -Lesser Key of Solomon

Notes: Image from the Dictionnaire Infernal, sigil from the Lesser Key of Solomon.

**Bifrons**

Bifrons, or Bifröus, or Bifrovs. He is an Earl, and appeareth in the Form of a Monster; but after a while, at the Command of the Exorcist, he putteth on the shape of a Man. His Office is to make one knowing in Astrology, Geometry, and other Arts and Sciences. He teacheth the Virtues of Precious Stones and Woods. He changeth Dead Bodies, and putteth them in another place; also he lighteth seeming Candles upon the Graves of the Dead. He hath under his Command 6 Legions of Spirits. His Seal is this, which he will own and submit unto, etc -Lesser Key of Solomon

Notes: Image from the Dictionnaire Infernal, sigil from the Lesser Key of Solomon.

**Botis**

Botis, a Great President, and an Earl. He appeareth at the first show in the form of an ugly Viper, then at the command of the Magician he putteth on a Human shape with Great Teeth, and two Horns, carrying a bright and sharp Sword in his hand. He telleth all things Past, and to Come, and reconcileth Friends and Foes. He ruleth over 60 Legions of Spirits, and this is his Seal, etc. -Lesser Key of Solomon

Notes: Sigil from the Lesser Key of Solomon, image by my art team.

**Brulefer**

Brulefer, who causes a person to be beloved of women. - The True Grimoire

Notes: This sigil was created by me, and it represents masculine energy (the points) reaching for the feminine (the circles). "A beautiful woman riding a dragon with three heads, mouths open as if roaring claws extended" was the vision I received. Image by my art team.

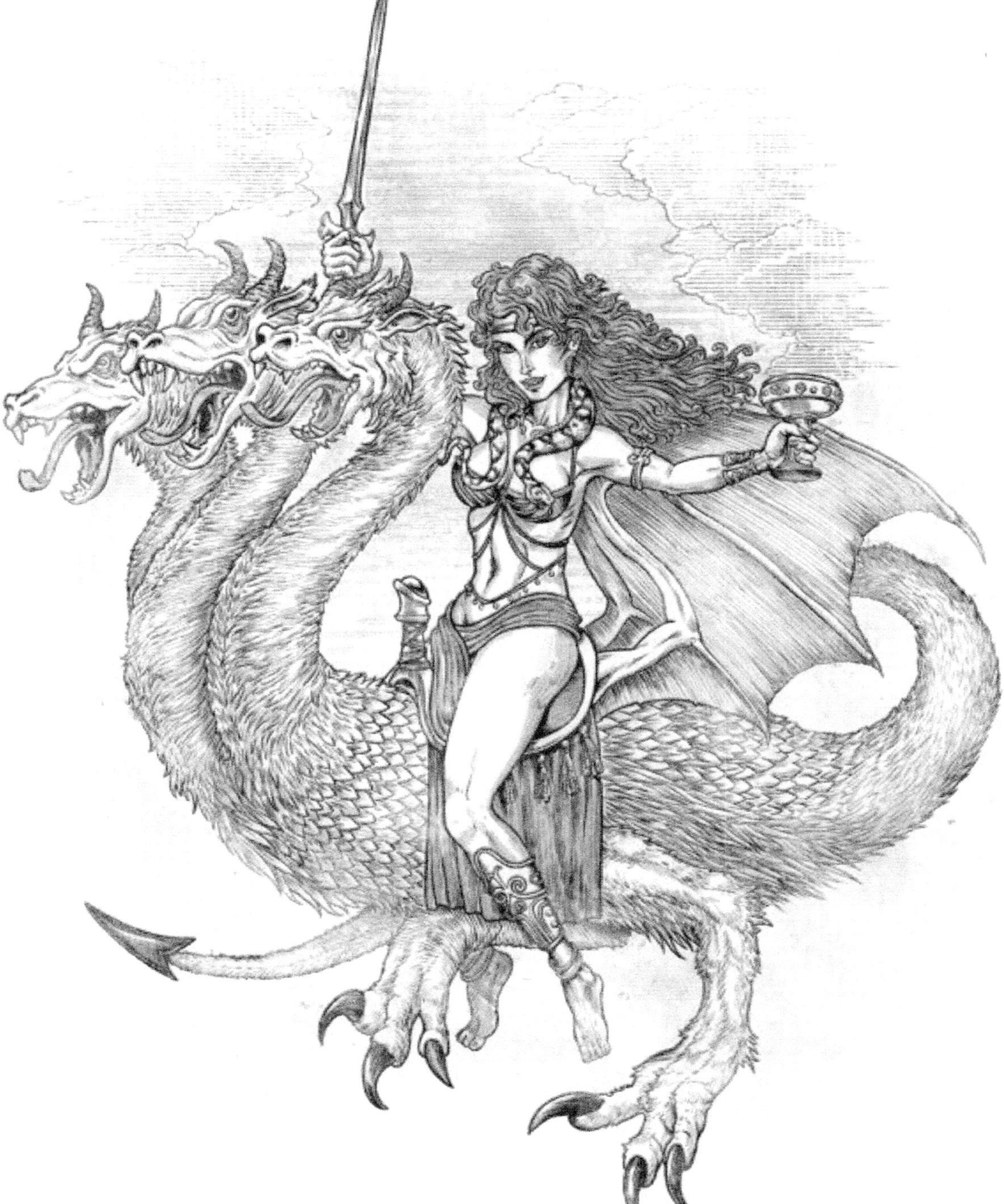

**Bucon**

Bucon, can cause hate and spiteful jealousy between members of the opposite sexes. - The Grimorium Verum

Notes: Sigil created by the author, the circle with the dot in the center represents the "eye of the mind" releasing the point, and the waves, and the smaller dots, which are meant to give the general feel of the mind experiencing jealousy. "A man and a woman walk down a street; the woman is yelling angrily at the man as a demon with great fangs and long fingernails demon looks on" is the image I received. Image drawn by my art team.

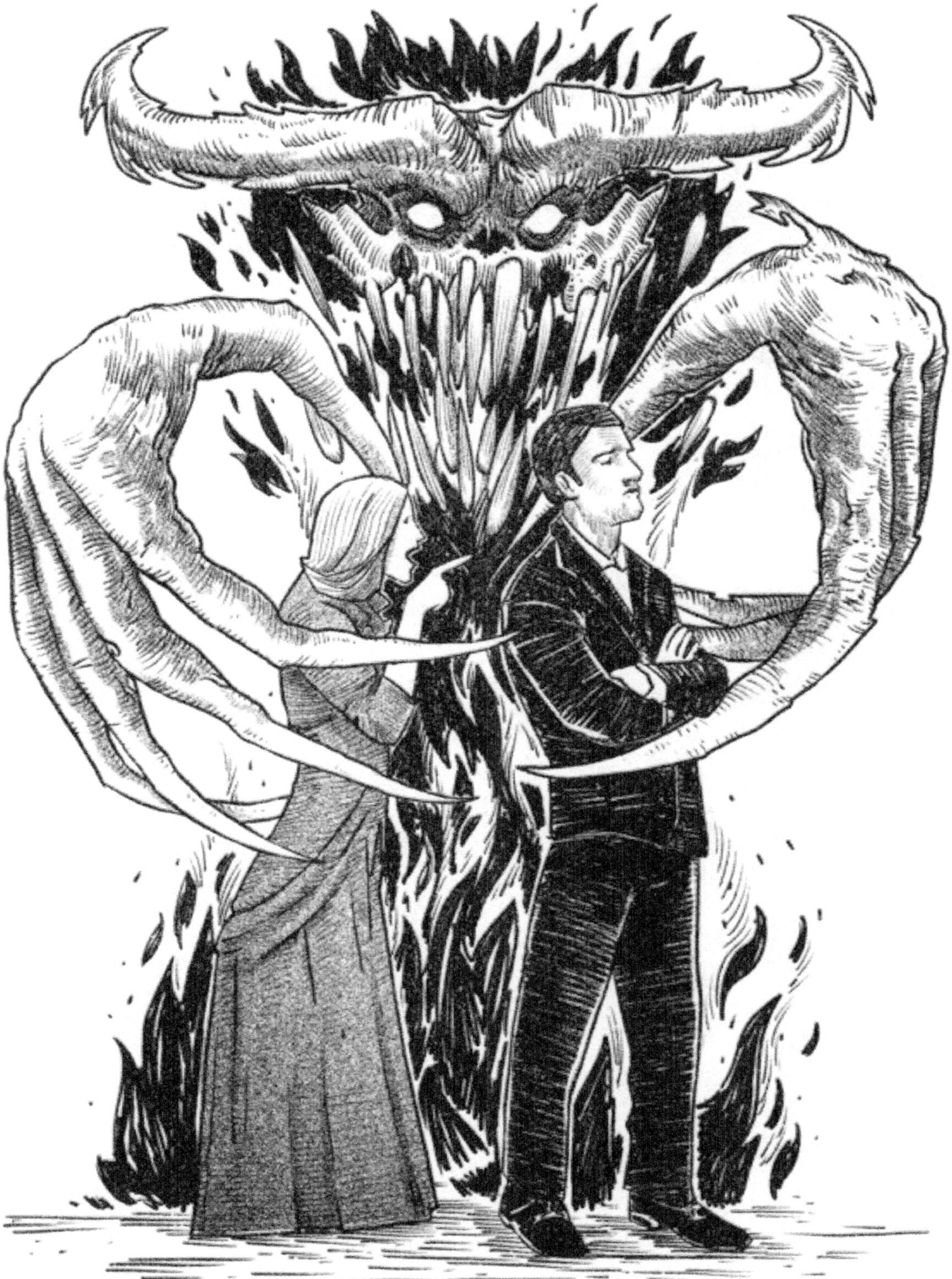

**Buer**

Buer, a Great President. He appeareth in Sagittary, and that is his shape when the Sun is there. He teaches Philosophy, both Moral and Natural, and the Logic Art, and also the Virtues of all Herbs and Plants. He healeth all distempers in man, and giveth good Familiars. He governeth 50 Legions of Spirits, and his Character of obedience is this, which thou must wear when thou callest him forth unto appearance. -Lesser Key of Solomon

Notes: Image from the Dictionnaire Infernal, sigil from the Lesser Key of Solomon.

## Bune

Buné (or Bim). He is a Strong, Great and Mighty Duke. He appeareth in the form of a Dragon with three heads, one like a Dog, one like a Gryphon, and one like a Man. He speaketh with a high and comely Voice. He changeth the Place of the Dead, and causeth the Spirits which be under him to gather together upon your Sepulchres. He giveth Riches unto a Man, and maketh him Wise and Eloquent. He giveth true Answers unto Demands. And he governeth 30 Legions of Spirits. His Seal is this, unto the which he oweth Obedience. -Lesser Key of Solomon. Notes: Sigil from the Lesser Key of Solomon, image by my art team.

**Camio**

Camio, or Caïm. He is a Great President, and appeareth in the Form of the Bird called a Thrush at first, but afterwards he putteth on the Shape of a Man carrying in his Hand a Sharp Sword. He seemeth to answer in Burning Ashes, or in Coals of Fire. He is a Good Disputer. His Office is to give unto Men the Under-standing of all Birds, Lowing of Bullocks, Barking of Dogs, and other Creatures; and also of the Voice of the Waters. He giveth True Answers of Things to Come. He was of the Order of Angels, but now ruleth over 30 Legions of Spirits Infernal. His Seal is this, which wear thou, etc. -Lesser Key of Solomon

Notes: Image from the Dictionnaire Infernal, sigil from the Lesser Key of Solomon.

**Cimejes or Kimaris**

Cimejes, or Cimeies, or Kimaris. He is a Marquis, Mighty, Great, Strong and Powerful, appearing like a Valiant Warrior riding upon a goodly Black Horse. He ruleth over all Spirits in the parts of Africa. His Office is to teach perfectly Grammar, Logic, Rhetoric, and to discover things Lost or Hidden, and Treasures. He governeth 20 Legions of Infernals; and his Seal is this, etc. -Lesser Key of Solomon

Notes: Image by my art team, sigil from the Lesser Key of Solomon.

## Claunech

Clauneck has power over riches, can cause treasures to be found. He can give great riches to he who makes a pact with him, for he is much loved by Lucifer. It is he who causes money to be brought. - Grimorium Verum

Notes: Sigils from the Secrets of Solomon and The Grimorium Verum. Illustration of Clauneck from the 1863 Dictionnaire Infernal.

## Clisthert

Clisthert allows you to have day or night, whichever you wish, when you desire either. - Grimorium Verum

Notes: Sigil from The Grimorium Verum. "A man with the scene split in half on one side of him is day, and on the other side is night. One side his face is like a man, with a bird wing on his shoulder, and on another side his face becomes demonic with a demon horn, and a bat wing on that shoulder. On the day side there is a sun and on the night side there is a moon." Image drawn by my art team.

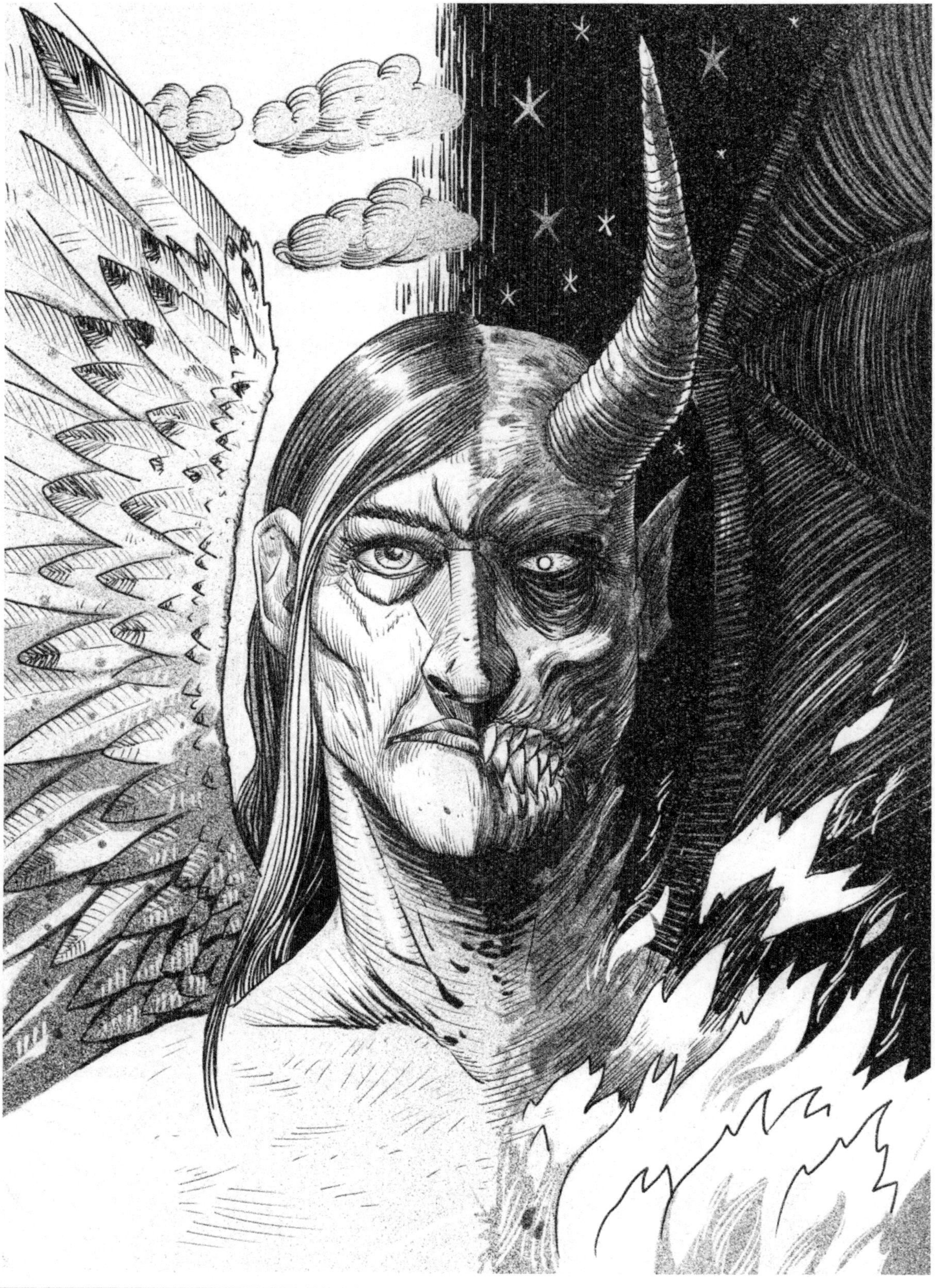

# Crocell

Crocell, or Crokel. He appeareth in the Form of an Angel. He is a Duke Great and Strong, speaking something Mystically of Hidden Things. He teacheth the Art of Geometry and the Liberal Sciences. He, at the Command of the Exorcist, will produce Great Noises like the Rushings of many Waters, although there be none. He warmeth Waters, and discovereth Baths. He was of the Order of Potestates, or Powers, before his fall, as he declared unto the King Solomon. He governeth 48 Legions of Spirits. His Seal is this, the which wear thou as aforesaid. -Lesser Key of Solomon

Notes: Image by my art team, sigil from the Lesser Key of Solomon.

**Dantalion**

Dantalion. He is a Duke Great and Mighty, appearing in the Form of a Man with many Countenances, all Men's and Women's Faces; and he hath a Book in his right hand. His Office is to teach all Arts and Sciences unto any; and to declare the Secret Counsels of any one; for he knoweth the Thoughts of all Men and Women, and can change them at his Will. He can cause Love, and show the Similitude of any person, and show the same by a Vision, let them be in what part of the World they Will. He governeth 36 Legions of Spirits; and this is his Seal, which wear thou, etc. -Lesser Key of Solomon

Notes: Image by my art team, sigil from the Lesser Key of Solomon.

**Decarabia**

Decarabia. He appeareth in the Form of a Star in a Pentacle at first; but after, at the command of the Exorcist, he putteth on the Image of a Man. His Office is to discover the Virtues of Birds and Precious Stones, and to make the Similitude of all kinds of Birds to fly before the Exorcist, singing and drinking as natural Birds do. He governeth 30 Legions of Spirits, being himself a Great Marquis. And this is his Seal, which is to be worn, etc -Lesser Key of Solomon. Notes: Sigil from the Lesser Key of Solomon, image by my art team.

# Egyn

Egyn Rex, is of the North, and appeareth in the likeness of a man, and his face is very clear, his nostrils are very sharp like a sword, & out of his mouth cometh flames of fire, and he rideth upon a dragon and he is crowned with a crown of precious stones, and in his cheeks he beareth 2 tuskes, and he beareth one his right side 2 hissing serpents shining and he cometh with a great noise and clamor before him go sundry kinds of musical Instruments and sweet organs, and he teacheth perfectly all physic, and singing, and the art Notaria, and the art of Nigromancy and the art memoratiuia, and he speaketh of 69 diverse parts of the world, and of things to come past and present, and of certain secrets, and hid things, and of the being and compacting of this world, and what the earth is, and whether the water may sustain the earth or the earth the water, and he telleth what a bottomless pit is called commonly Abissus, and where it is, and what the wine is, and from whence it commeth, and he giveth very good acquaintance and dignities, prelateships and confirmeth the same, and maketh consecration of books and other things and giveth true answers of all questions and demands and thou must look to the North when thou callest him, and so soon as he appeareth, shewe him Sigillum Salomonis, and his ring and forthwith he will fall down, to the earth, and will worship the master and the master shall take and thank him therefore, and he hath 12000 legions, and causeth a man to win at all manner of games, and Rodabell, vel Radabelbes, be the messengers of the king of the North - The Book of Oberon. Notes: Image by my art team, sigil from the grimoire Fasciculus Rerum Geomanticarum.

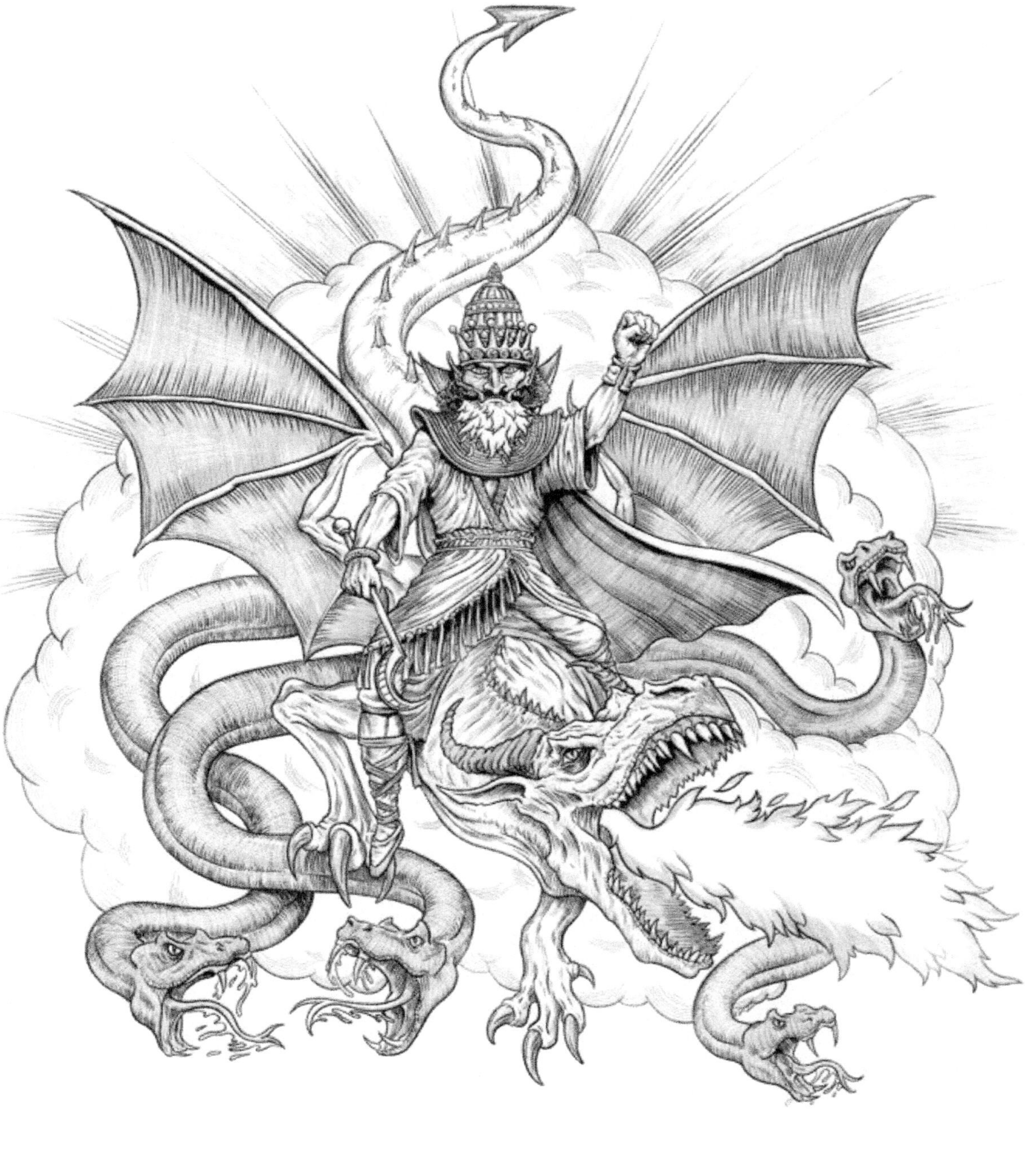

**Elelogap**

Agalierept and Tarchimache (Lucifuge Rofocale) are the rulers of Elelogap, who in turn governs matters connected with water. - The Grimorium Verum

Notes: We have little to go on concerning the nature of this spirit. My feeling on this one is that it is something like the fish god Dagon. I created this sigil after invoking the spirit. The sigil symbolizes a half man/half fish god, rising from the waves. Image by my art team.

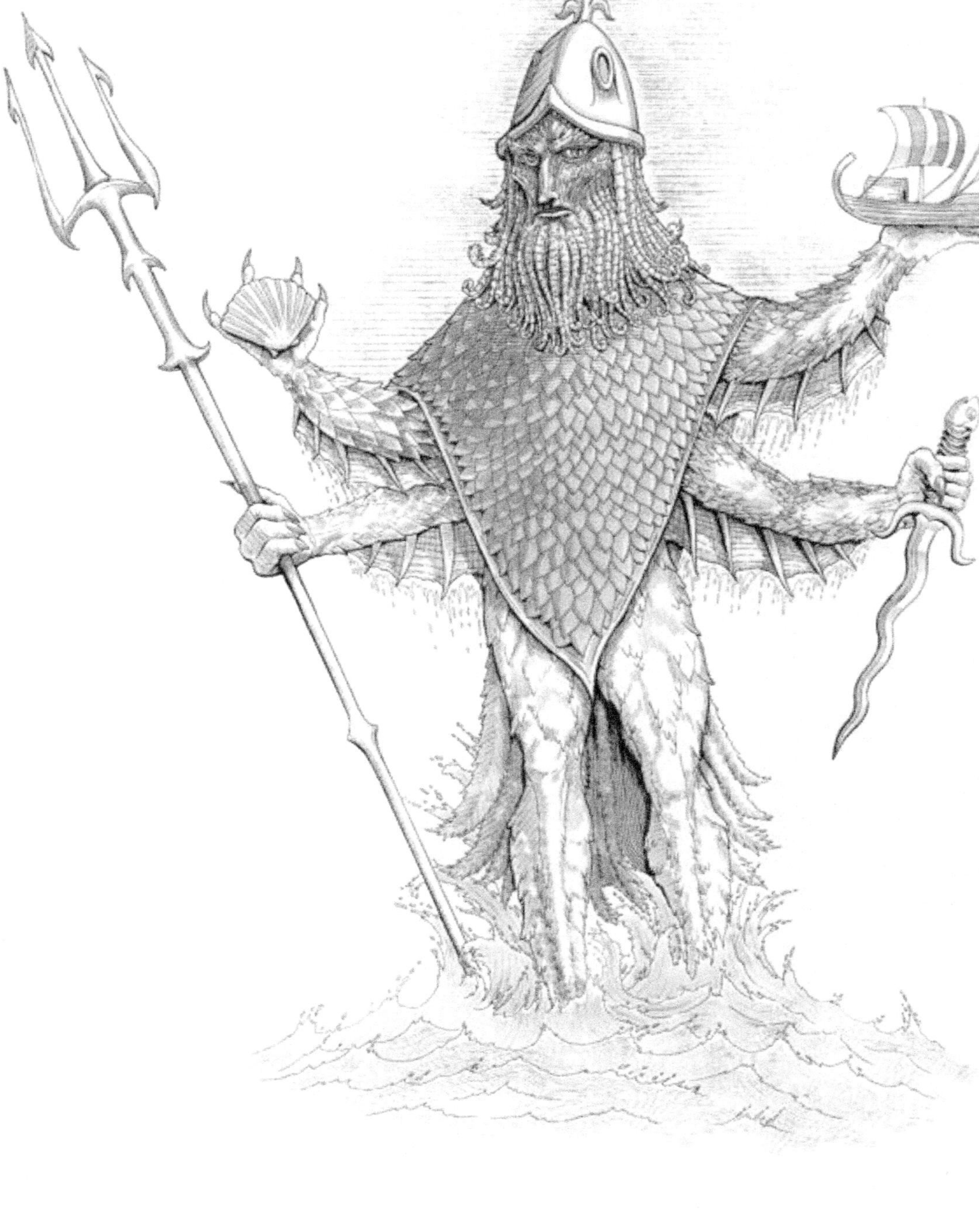

**Eligos**

Eligos, a Great Duke, appeareth in the form of a goodly Knight, carrying a Lance, an Ensign, and a Serpent. He discovereth hidden things, and knoweth things to come; and of Wars, and how the Soldiers will or shall meet. He causeth the Love of Lords and Great Persons. He governeth 60 Legions of Spirits. His Seal is this, etc. - Lesser Key of Solomon.

Notes: Image from the Dictionnaire Infernal, sigil from the Lesser Key of Solomon.

**Fleurety**

The Lieutenant General Fleurety, who has the power to perform any task he wishes during the night. He can also cause hail or raise a storm where he wishes. He commands a very considerable army of spirits, and he has under him Bathim, Parsan and Abigar. - The Grand Grimoire.

Notes: Sigil from The Grand Grimoire, image by my art team.

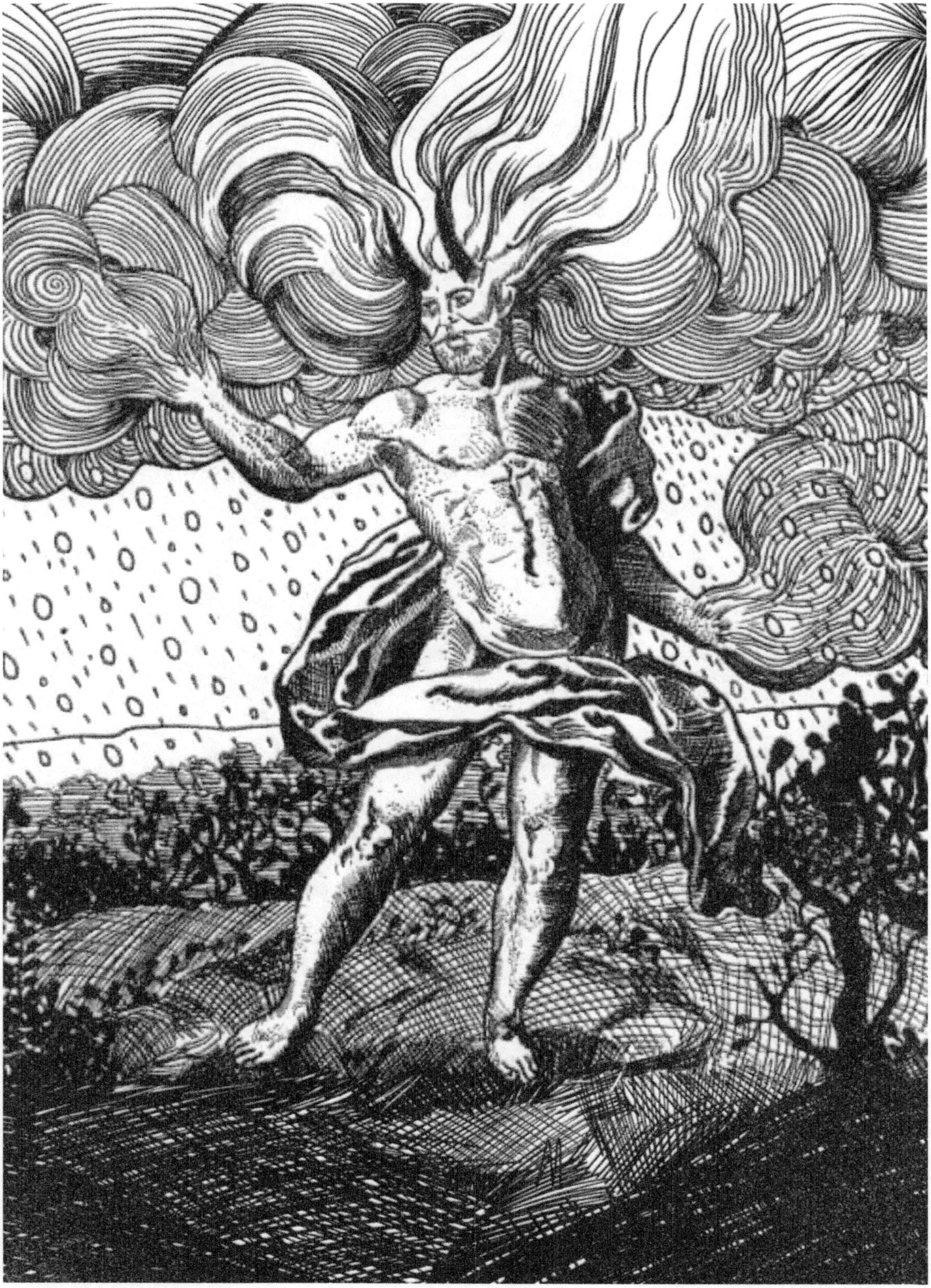

## Focalor

Focalor, or Forcalor, or Furcalor. He is a Mighty Duke and Strong. He appeareth in the Form of a Man with Gryphon's Wings. His office is to slay Men, and to drown them in the Waters, and to overthrow Ships of War, for he hath Power over both Winds and Seas; but he will not hurt any man or thing if he be commanded to the contrary by the Exorcist. He also hath hopes to return to the Seventh Throne after 1,000 years. He governeth 30 Legions of Spirits, and his Seal is this, etc. -Lesser Key of Solomon.

Notes: Image by my art team, sigil from the Lesser Key of Solomon.

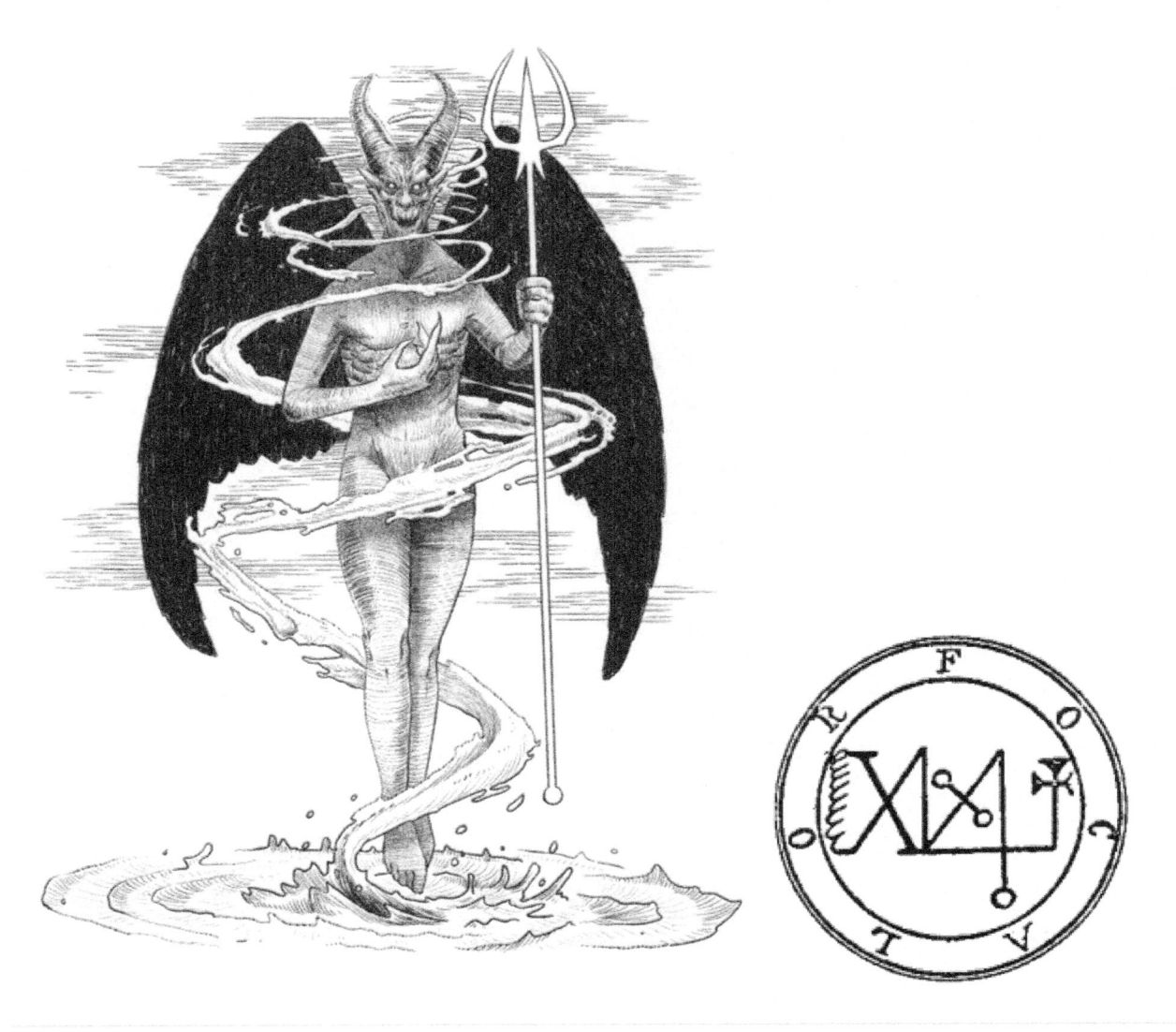

## Foras

Foras. He is a Mighty President, and appeareth in the Form of a Strong Man in Human Shape. He can give the understanding to Men how they may know the Virtues of all Herbs and Precious Stones. He teacheth the Arts of Logic and Ethics in all their parts. If desired he maketh men invisible, and to live long, and to be eloquent. He can discover Treasures and recover things Lost. He ruleth over 29 Legions of Spirits, and his Seal is this, which wear thou, etc.

**Forneus**

Forneus. He is a Mighty and Great Marquis, and appeareth in the Form of a Great Sea-Monster. He teacheth, and maketh men wonderfully knowing in the Art of Rhetoric. He causeth men to have a Good Name, and to have the knowledge and understanding of Tongues. He maketh one to be beloved of his Foes as well as of his Friends. He governeth 29 Legions of Spirits, partly of the Order of Thrones, and partly of that of Angels. His Seal is this, which wear thou, etc. -Lesser Key of Solomon. Notes: Image by my art team, sigil from the Lesser Key of Solomon.

**Frimost**

Frimost has power over women and girls and will help you to obtain their use. - The Grimorium Verum

Notes: Sigils from The Grimorium Verum and the Secrets of Solomon. The Grimoire of Honorius says that he should be invoked on a Tuesday, the first stone one finds should be given him, and that he is to be treated with dignity and honor. He is also called Nambroth in some editions of The Grimoire of Honorius. MS 4666 says that he appears as a Satyr. Image of the demon drawn by my art team.

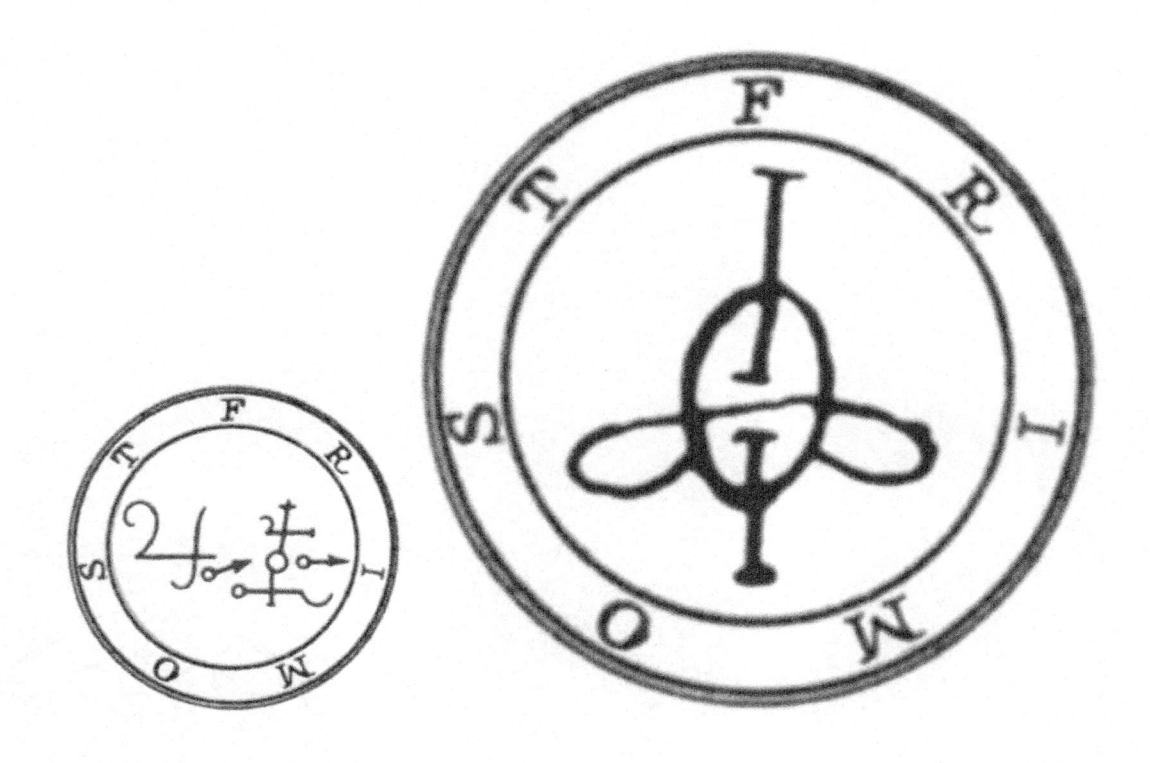

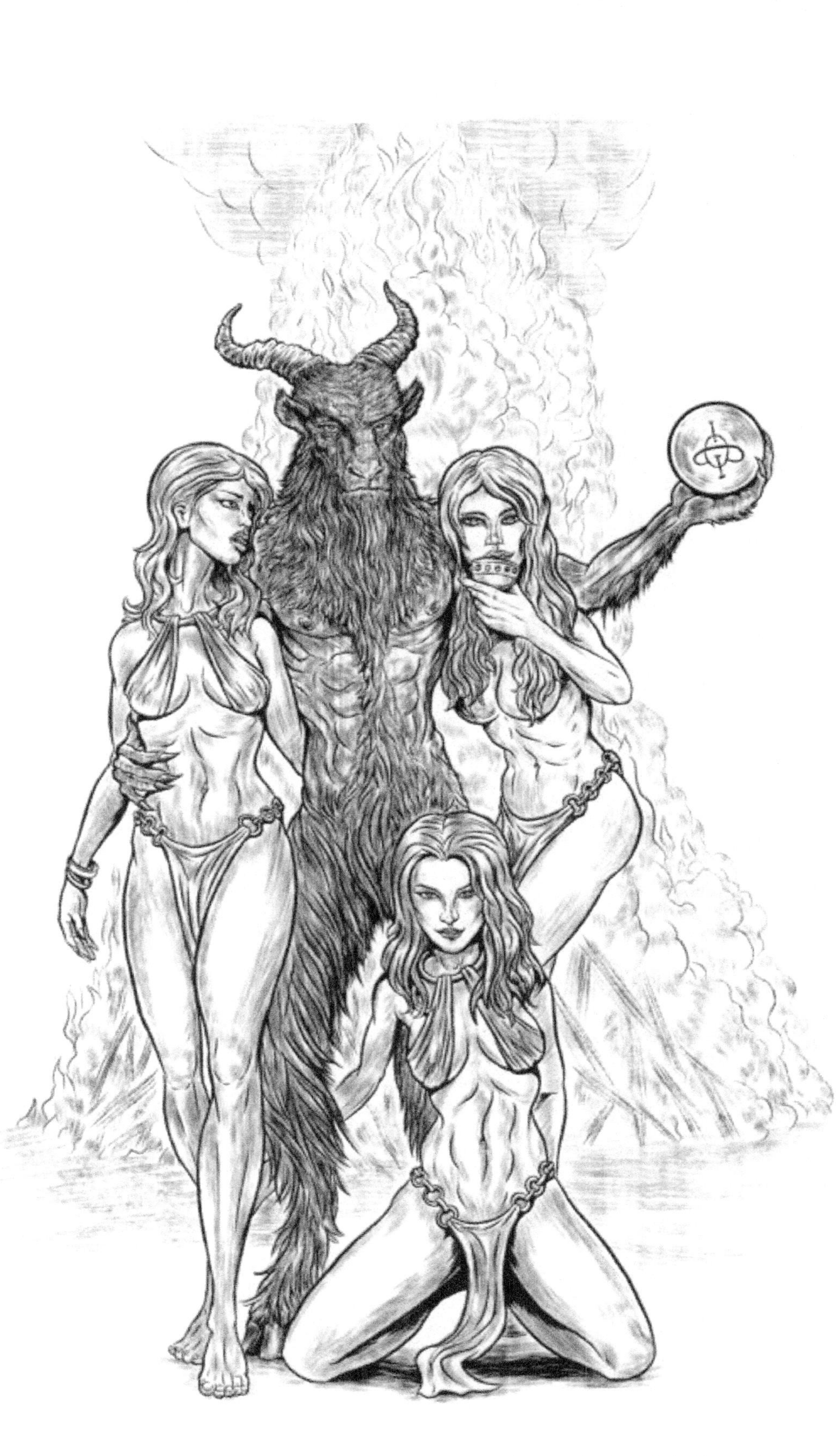

**Frucissiere**

Frucissiere revives the dead. - The Grimorium Verum

Notes: Sigil from the Grimorium Verum, Image by my art team.

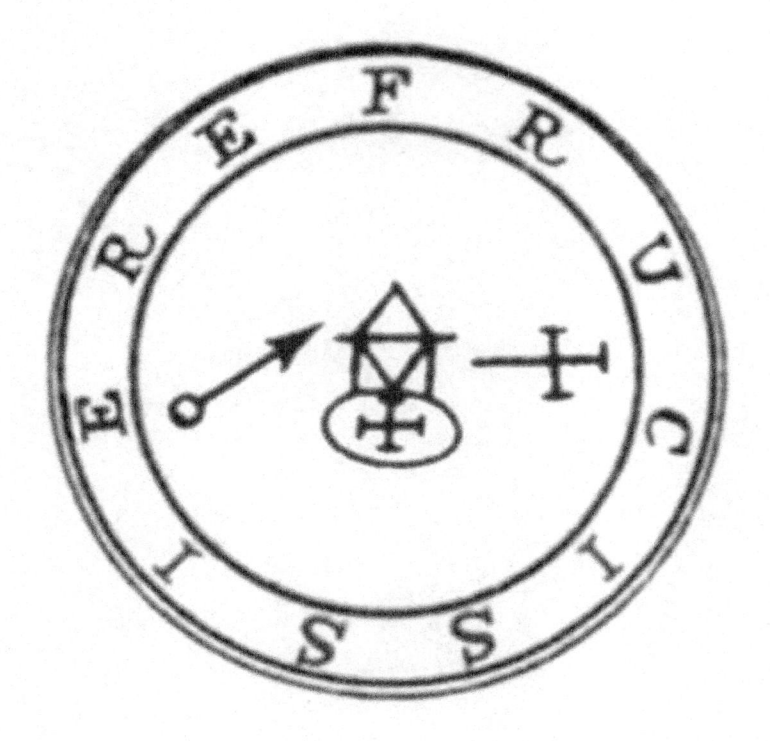

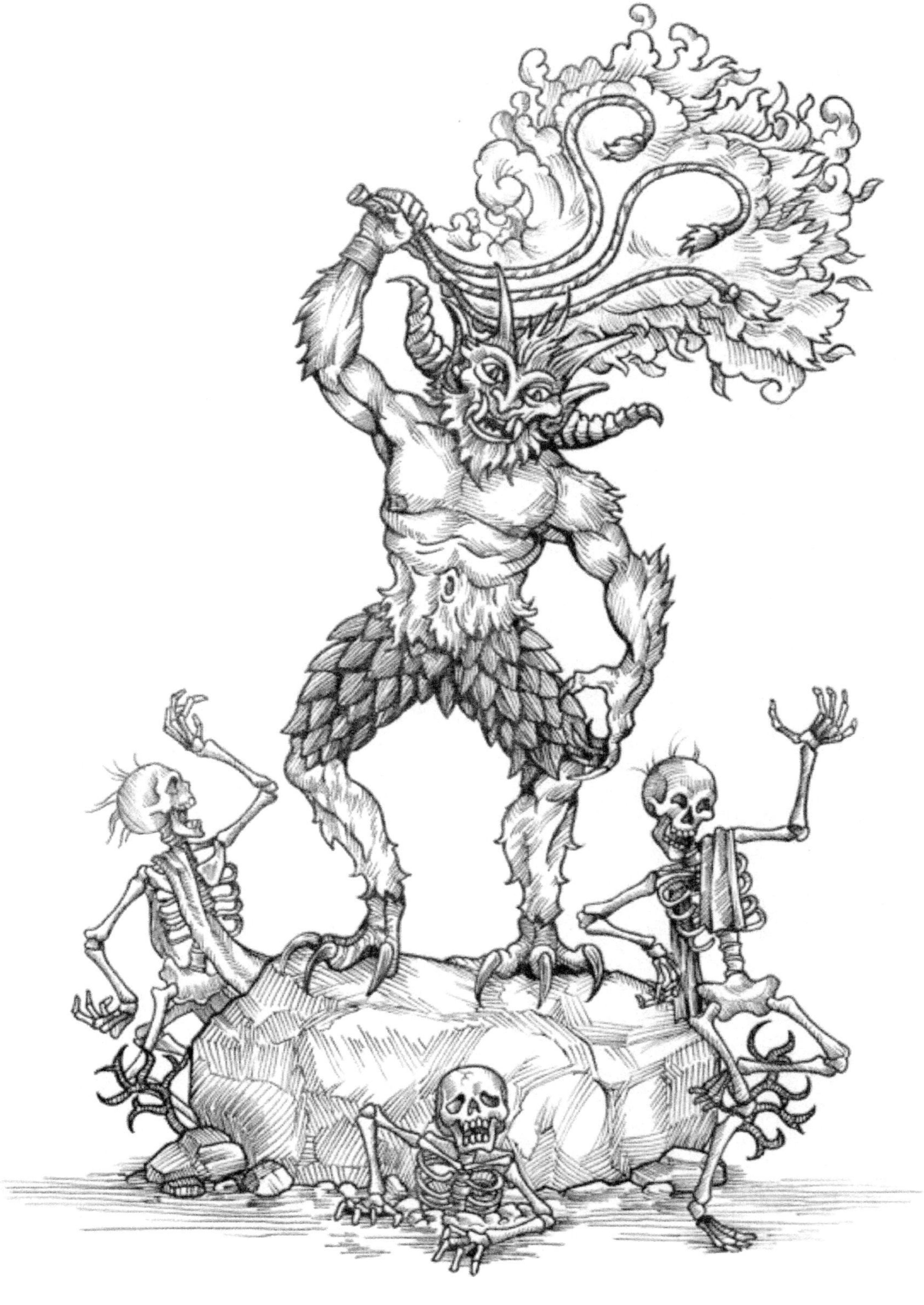

**Frutimierre**

Frutimiere prepares all kinds of feasts for you. - The True Grimoire

Notes: sigil from the Grimorium Verum, image by my art team.

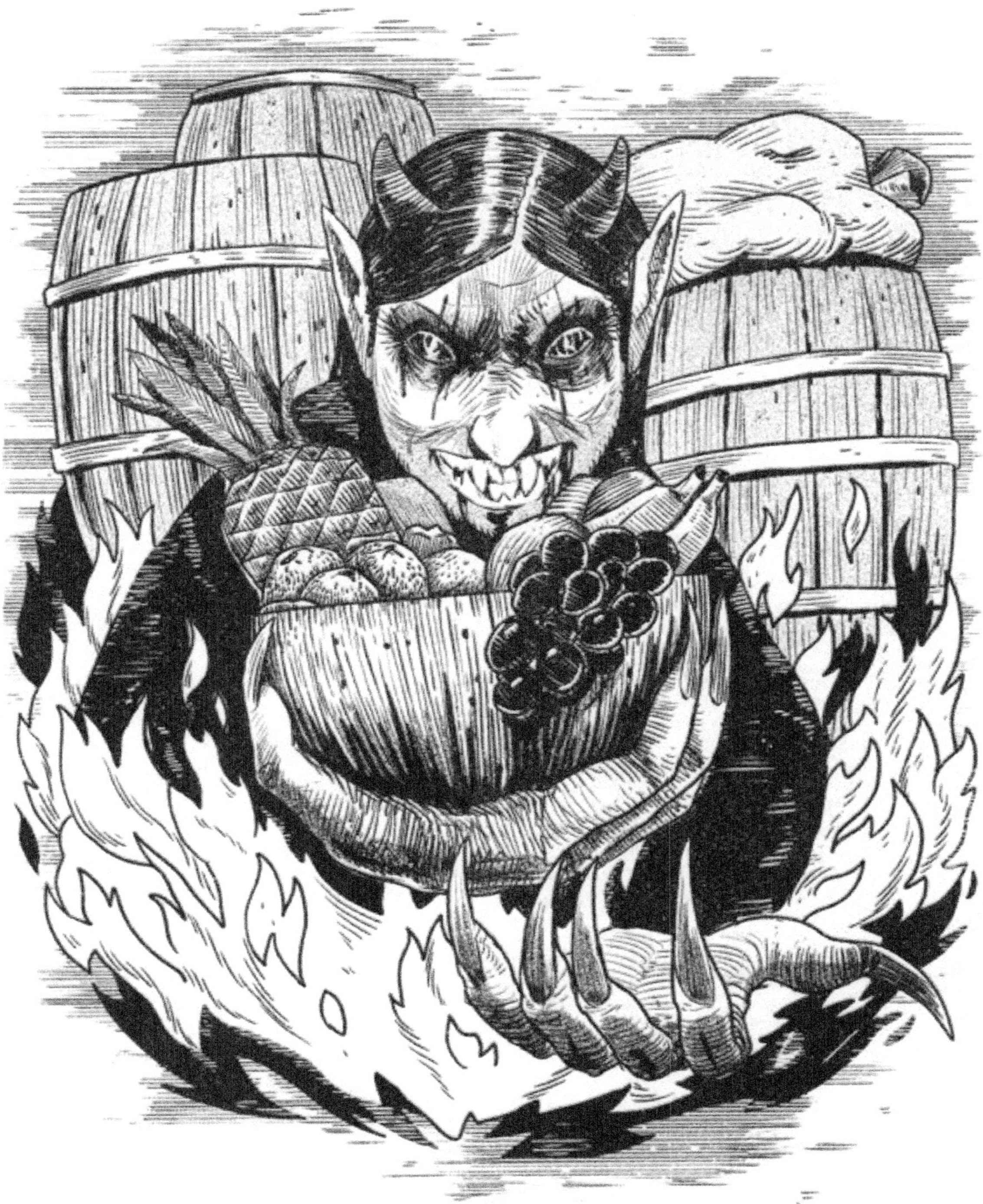

## Furcas

Furcas. He is a Knight, and appeareth in the Form of a Cruel Old Man with a long Beard and a hoary Head, riding upon a pale-coloured Horse, with a Sharp Weapon in his hand. His Office is to teach the Arts of Philosophy, Astrology, Rhetoric, Logic, Cheiromancy, and Pyromancy, in all their parts, and perfectly. He hath under his Power 20 Legions of Spirits. His Seal, or Mark, is thus made, etc. -Lesser Key of Solomon

Notes: Image from the Dictionnaire Infernal, sigil from the Lesser Key of Solomon.

**Furfur**

Furfur. He is a Great and Mighty Earl, appearing in the Form of an Hart with a Fiery Tail. He never speaketh truth unless he be compelled, or brought up within a triangle, Δ. Being therein, he will take upon himself the Form of an Angel. Being bidden, he speaketh with a hoarse voice. Also he will wittingly urge Love between Man and Woman. He can raise Lightnings and Thunders, Blasts, and Great Tempestuous Storms. And he giveth True Answers both of Things Secret and Divine, if commanded. He ruleth over 26 Legions of Spirits. And his Seal is this, etc -Lesser Key of Solomon

Notes: Image from the Dictionnaire Infernal, sigil from the Lesser Key of Solomon.

# Gaap

Gäap. He is a Great President and a Mighty Prince. He appeareth when the Sun is in some of the Southern Signs, in a Human Shape, going before Four Great and Mighty Kings, as if he were a Guide to conduct them along on their way. His Office is to make men Insensible or Ignorant; as also in Philosophy to make them Knowing, and in all the Liberal Sciences. He can cause Love or Hatred, also he can teach thee to consecrate those things that belong to the Dominion of AMAYMON his King. He can deliver Familiars out of the Custody of other Magicians, and answereth truly and perfectly of things Past, Present, and to Come. He can carry and re-carry men very speedily from one Kingdom to another, at the Will and Pleasure of the Exorcist. He ruleth over 66 Legions of Spirits, and he was of the Order of Potentates. His Seal is this to be made and to be worn as aforesaid, etc - Lesser Key of Solomon

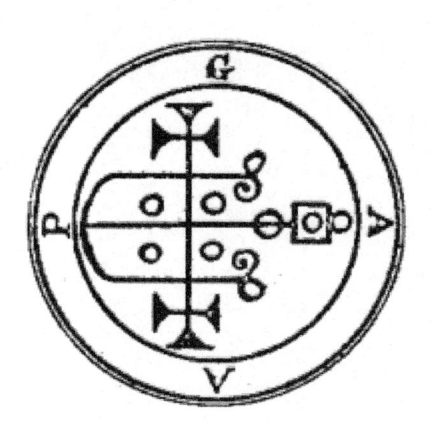

Notes: Image from the Dictionnaire Infernal, sigil from the Lesser Key of Solomon.

**Glasya-Labolas**

Glasya-Labolas. He is a Mighty President and Earl, and showeth himself in the form of a Dog with Wings like a Gryphon. He teacheth all Arts and Sciences in an instant and is an Author of Bloodshed and Manslaughter. He teacheth all things Past, and to Come. If desired, he causeth the love both of Friends and of Foes. He can make a Man to go Invisible. And he hath under his command 36 Legions of Spirits. His Seal is this, to be, etc. -Lesser Key of Solomon

Notes: Image from the Dictionnaire Infernal, sigil from the Lesser Key of Solomon.

**Gremory**

Gremory, or Gamori. He is a Duke Strong and Powerful, and appeareth in the Form of a Beautiful Woman, with a Duchess's Crown tied about her waist, and riding on a Great Camel. His Office is to tell of all Things Past, Present, and to Come; and of Treasures Hid, and what they lie in; and to procure the Love of Women both Young and Old. He governeth 26 Legions of Spirits, and his Seal is this, etc. -Lesser Key of Solomon

Notes: Image from the Dictionnaire Infernal, sigil from the Lesser Key of Solomon.

**Guland**

Guland causes all illnesses. - The Grimorium Verum

Notes: The Grimoire of Honorius says that he should be invoked on a Saturday and offered burned bread. Secrets of Solomon also notes that he has the power of healing.

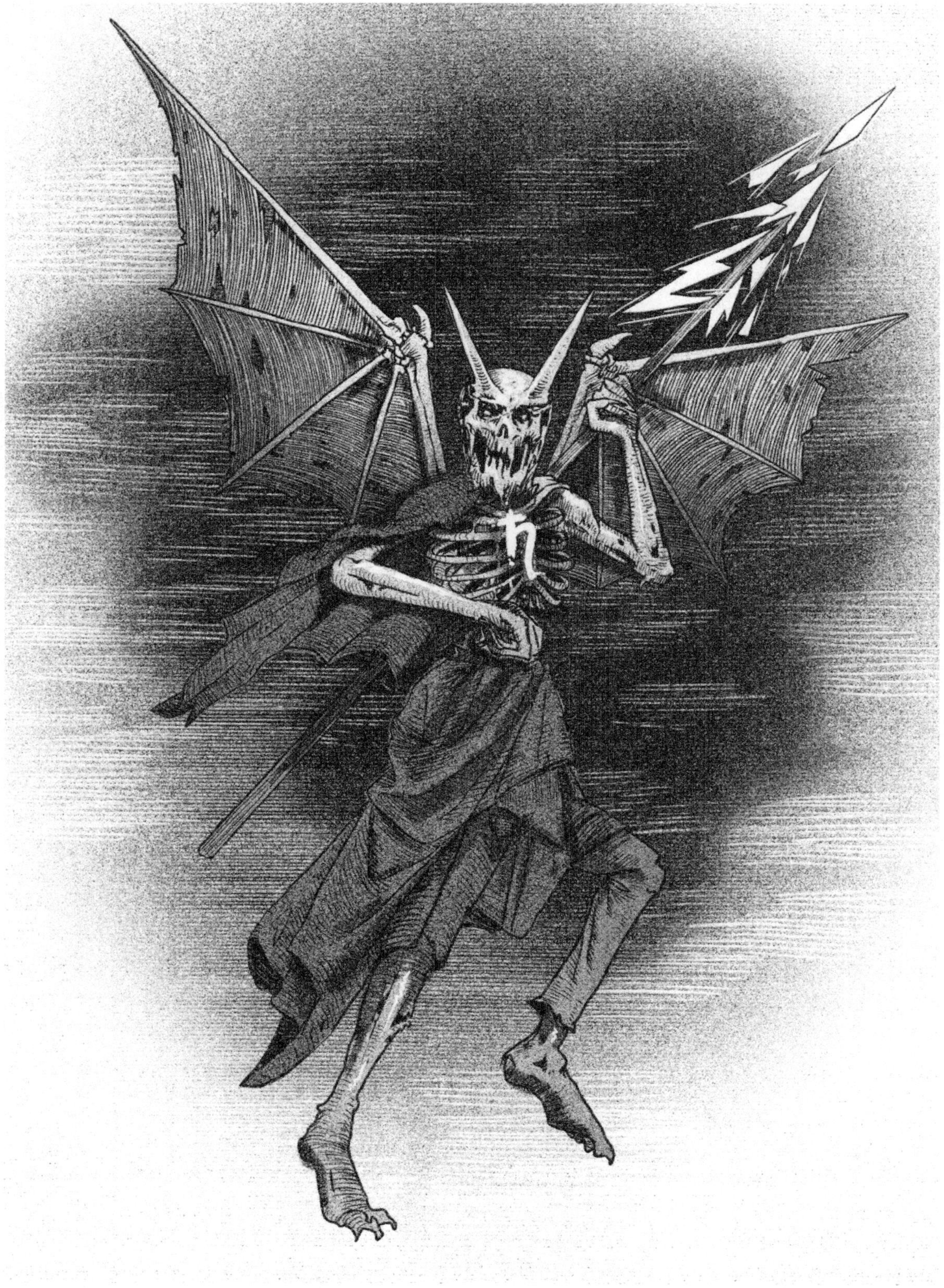

**Gusion**

Duke, called Gusion. He appeareth like a Xenopilus. He telleth all things, Past, Present, and to Come, and showeth the meaning and resolution of all questions thou mayest ask. He conciliateth and reconcileth friendships, and giveth Honour and Dignity unto any. He ruleth over 40 Legions of Spirits. His Seal is this, the which wear thou as aforesaid. -Lesser Key of Solomon

Notes: The Dictionnaire Infernal states that Gusion takes the form of a camel, so that is how I have shown him here. Sigil from the Lesser Key of Solomon.

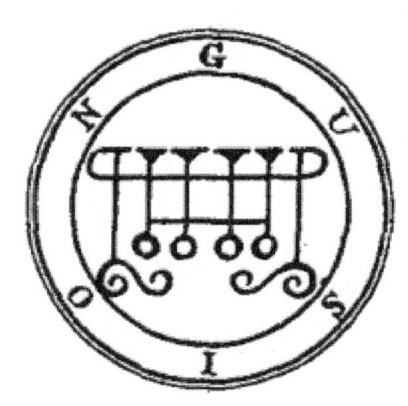

**Haagenti**

Haagenti. He is a President, appearing in the Form of a Mighty Bull with Gryphon's Wings. This is at first, but after, at the Command of the Exorcist he putteth on Human Shape. His Office is to make Men wise, and to instruct them in divers things; also to Transmute all Metals into Gold; and to change Wine into Water, and Water into Wine. He governeth 33 Legions of Spirits, and his Seal is this, etc. -Lesser Key of Solomon. Notes: Image by my art team, sigil from the Lesser Key of Solomon.

**Hael**

Hael enables anyone to speak in any language he wishes, and also, he teaches the means whereby any type of letter may be written. He is also able to teach those things which are most secret and completely hidden. – The Grimorium Verum

Notes: sigil from the Grimorium Verum. "A man holding a scroll on which is written four different languages or symbols, such as Greek, English, Hebrew, and Latin. He is in the form of an angel with wings and long robes. He looks fierce but not evil." Image by my art team.

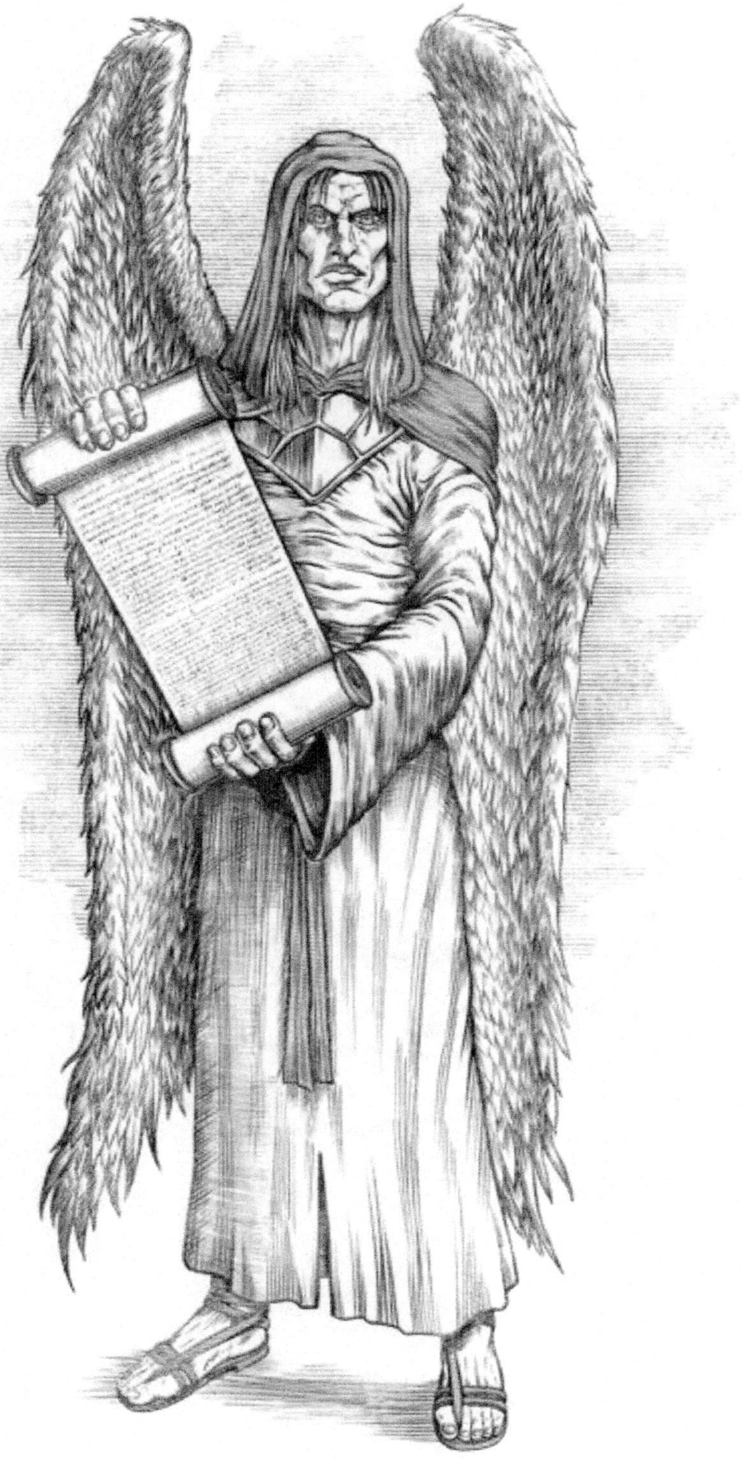

**Halphus**

Halphas, or Malthus (or Malthas). He is a Great Earl, and appeareth in the Form of a Stock-Dove. He speaketh with a hoarse Voice. His Office is to build up Towers, and to furnish them with Ammunition and Weapons, and to send Men-of-War to places appointed. He ruleth over 26 Legions of Spirits, and his Seal is this, etc. - Lesser Key of Solomon

Notes: Public domain image of a pigeon. Sigil from the Lesser Key of Solomon.

**Haristum**

Haristum, who can cause anyone to pass through fire without being touched by it.
- Grimorium Verum

Notes: Sigil created by me and represents the motion of a human (the circle), the line with the arrow, passing through flames. "Dragon in the fire with a crown on, breathing flames, with flames all around it" was the vision I received. Image by my art team.

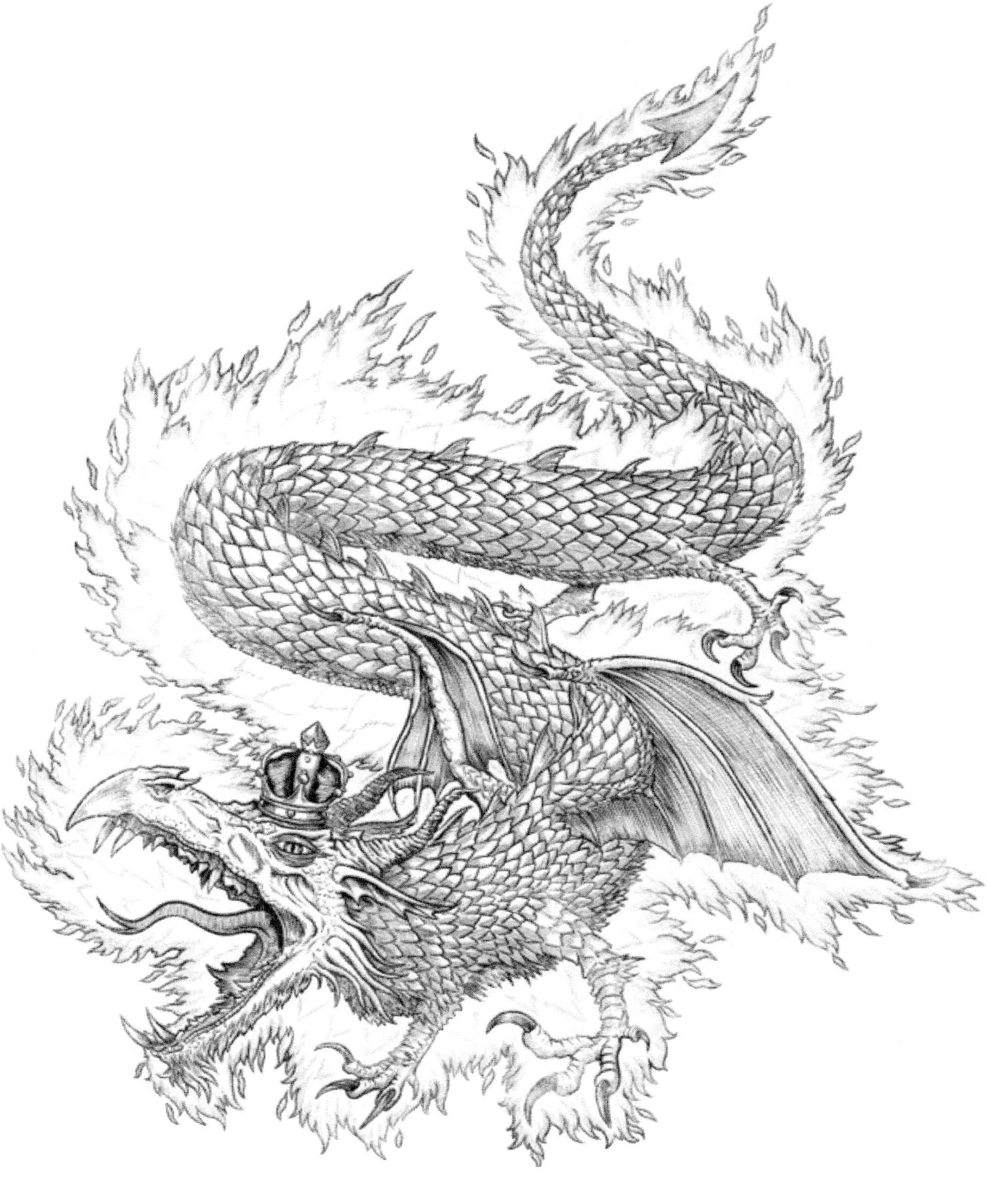

**Haures**

Haures, or Hauras, or Havres, or Flauros. He is a Great Duke, and appeareth at first like a Leopard, Mighty, Terrible, and Strong, but after a while, at the Command of the Exorcist, he putteth on Human Shape with Eyes Flaming and Fiery, and a most Terrible Countenance. He giveth True Answers of all things, Present, Past, and to Come. But if he be not commanded into a Triangle, Δ, he will Lie in all these Things, and deceive and beguile the Exorcist in these things or in such and such business. He will, lastly, talk of the Creation of the World, and of Divinity, and of how he and other Spirits fell. He destroyeth and burneth up those who be the Enemies of the Exorcist should he so desire it; also he will not suffer him to be tempted by any other Spirit or otherwise. He governeth 36 Legions of Spirits, and his Seal is this, to be worn as a Lamen, etc. -Lesser Key of Solomon

Notes. Image from the Dictionnaire Infernal, sigil from the Lesser Key of Solomon.

**Heramael**

Heramael teaches the art of healing, including the complete knowledge of any illness and its cure, He also makes known the virtues of plants, where they are to be found, when to pluck them, and their making into a complete cure. - The True Grimoire

Notes: I feel strongly that this spirit is feminine, a goddess, so that is how I asked the artist to draw her. Sigil from the Grimorium Verum.

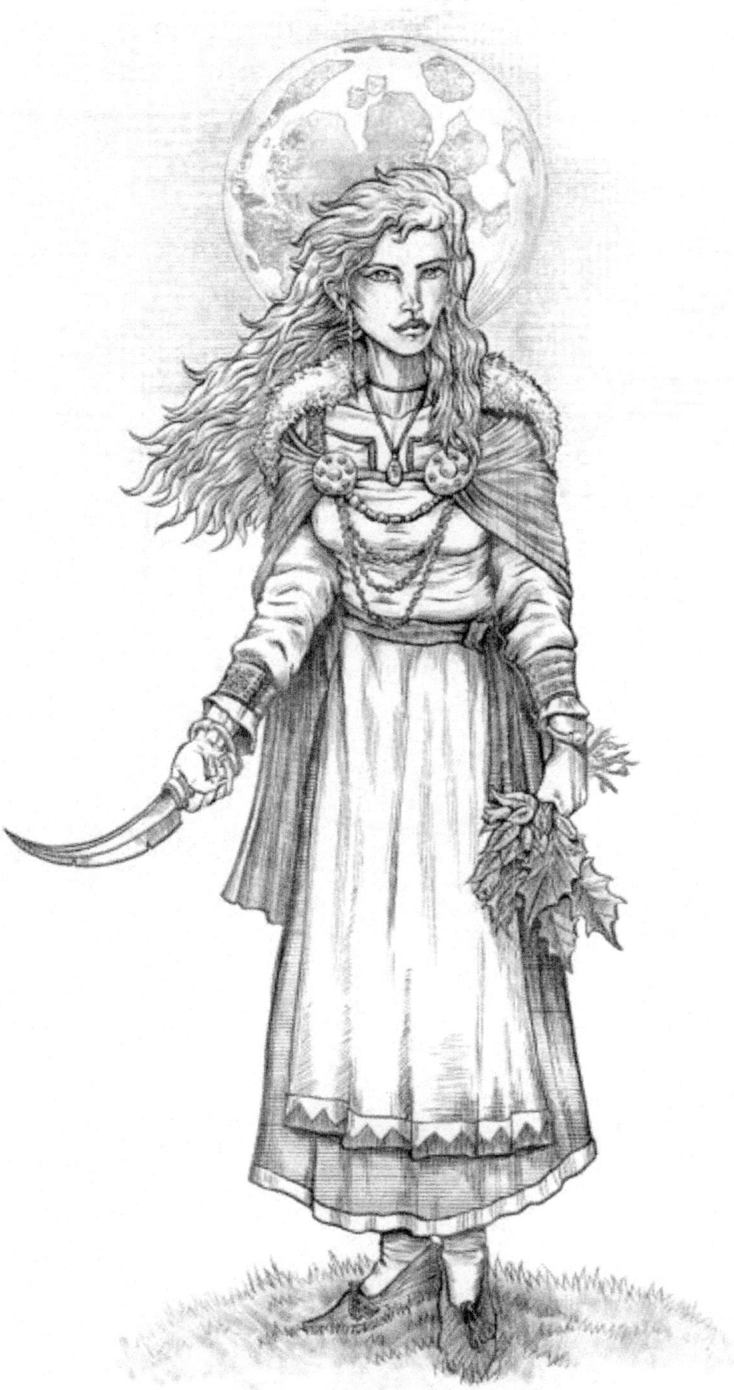

## Hicpacth

Hicpacth, or Hiepacth, will bring you a person in an instant, though he be far away. - Grimorium Verum

Notes: Sigil from the Grimorium Verum "A man standing on a large snake, the snake has its jaws open." Image by my art team.

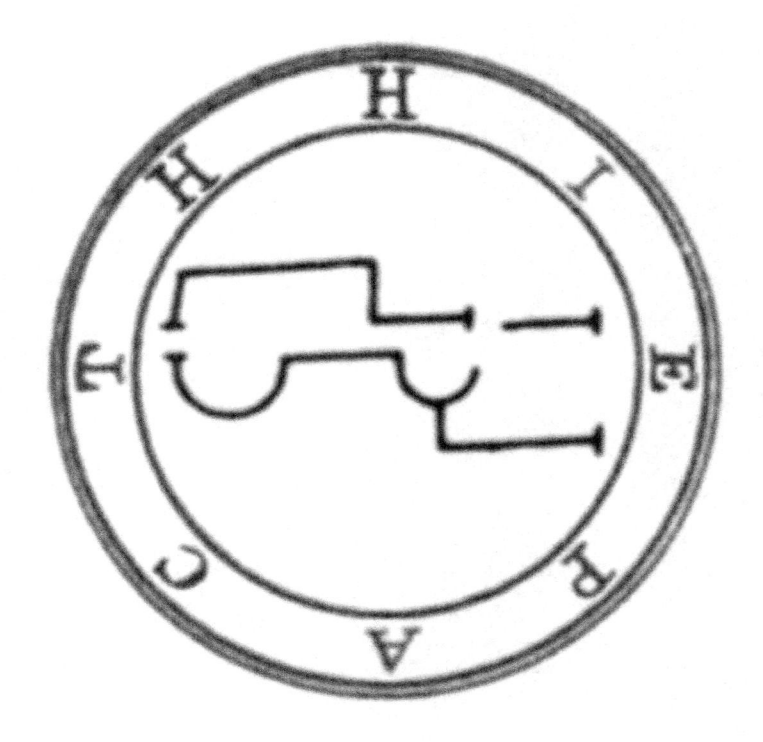

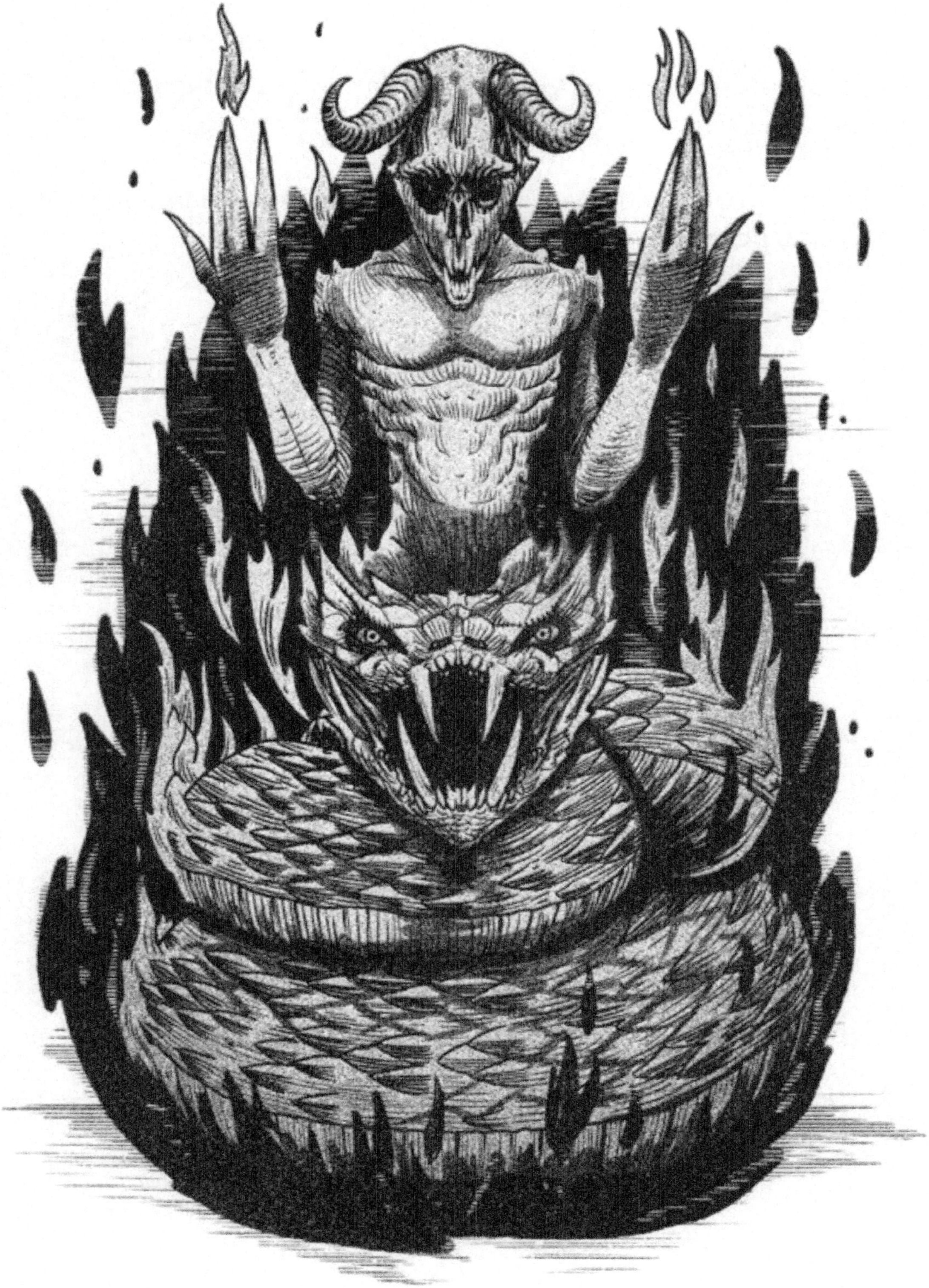

**Huictigaras**

Huictiigaras causes sleep in the case of some, and insomnia in others. - Grimorium Verum

Notes: sigil from the Grimorium Verum. "A two headed dragon lying on the ground. One head is asleep, and the other is raised up and awake and looking at the viewer," was the vision I received. Image by my art team.

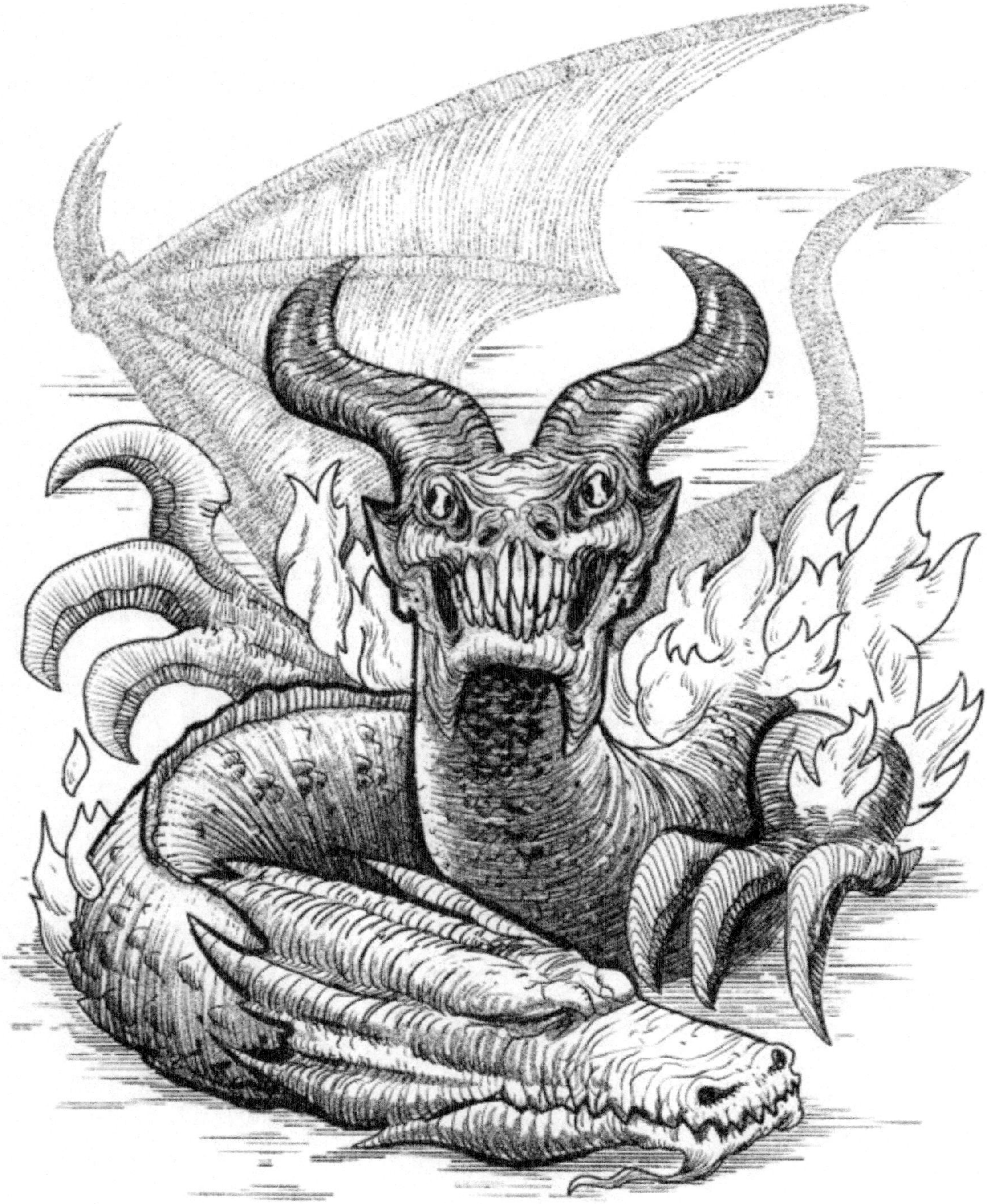

**Humots**

Humots can bring you any book you desire. - The True Grimoire

Notes: Sigil from the Grimorium Verum, image by Jenny Kelevra.

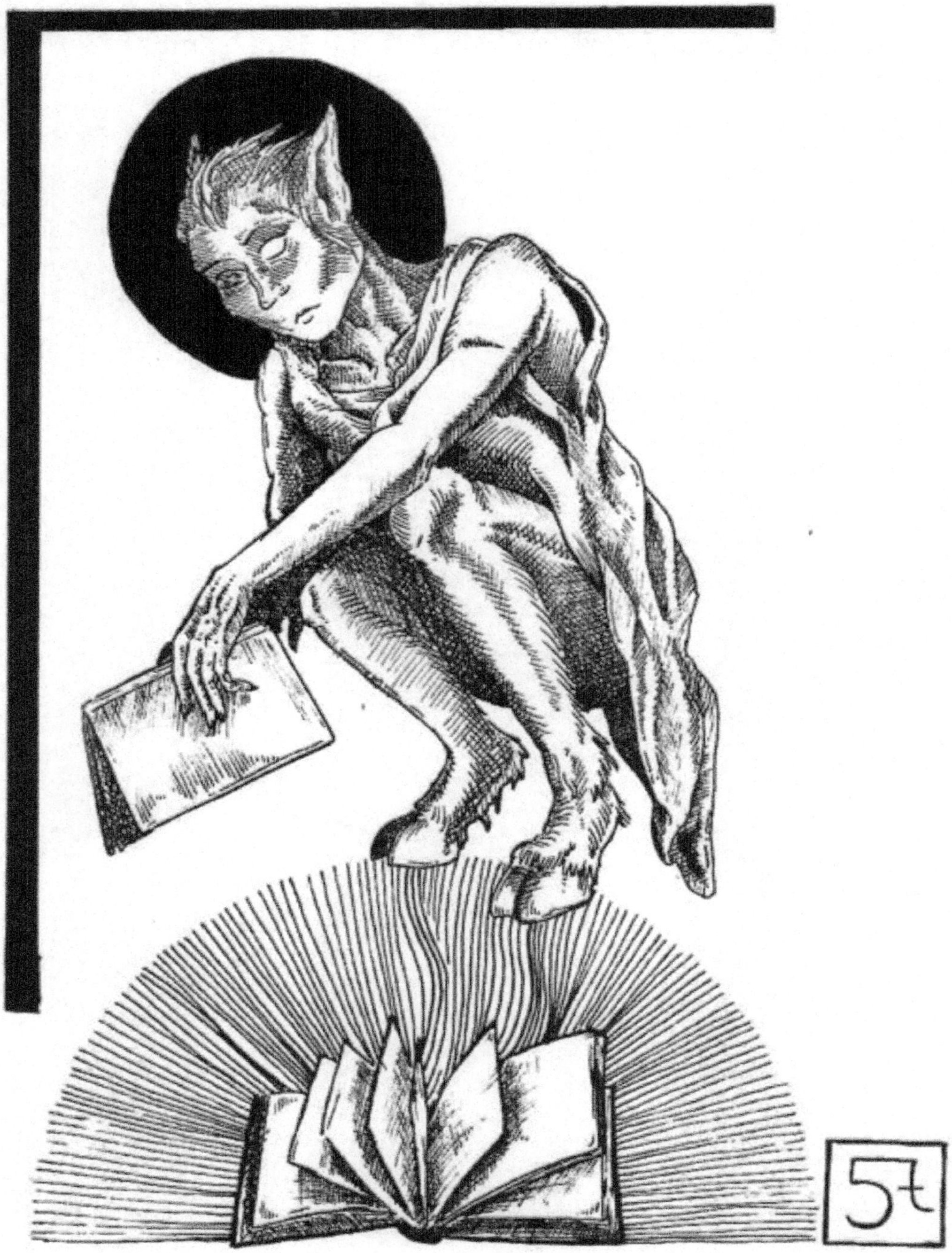

**Ipos**

Ipos. He is an Earl, and a Mighty Prince, and appeareth in the form of an Angel with a Lion's Head, and a Goose's Foot, and Hare's Tail. He knoweth all things Past, Present, and to Come. He maketh men witty and bold. He governeth 36 Legions of Spirits. His Seal is this, which thou shalt wear, etc. -Lesser Key of Solomon

Notes: Image from the Dictionnaire Infernal, sigil from the Lesser Key of Solomon.

**Khil**

Khil makes great earthquakes. - The True Grimoire

Notes: Sigil from The Grimorium Verum Notes: Illustration by Matti Sinkkonen "a lion headed snake, roaring. cracks opening in the earth showing his power to create earthquakes." Image by my art team.

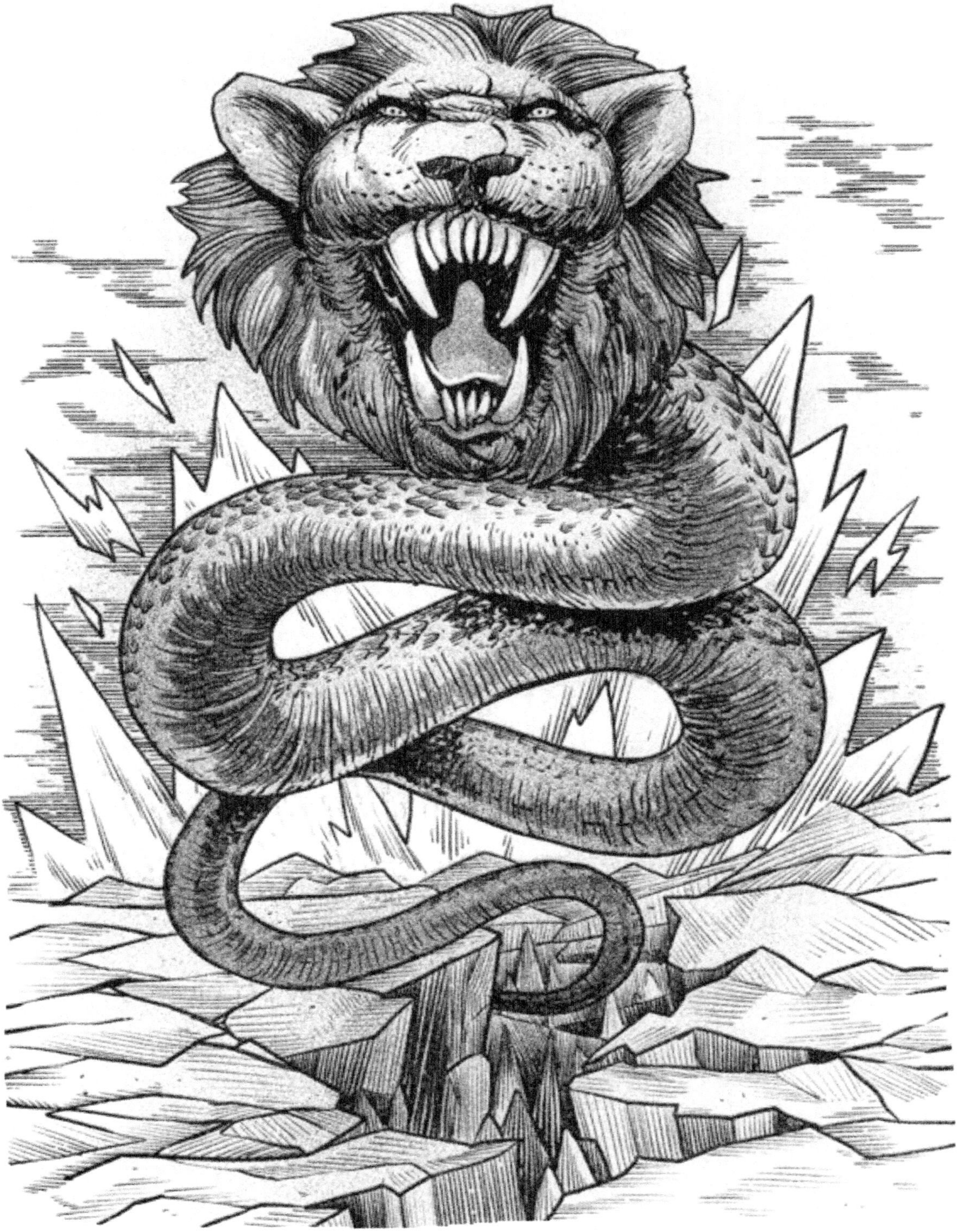

## Klepoth

Klepoth makes you see all sorts of dreams and visions. - The Grimorium Verum

Notes: Sigils from The Grimorium Verum and the Secrets of Solomon. "A demon holding and looking into a large crystal ball the size and a great battle being shown in the ball." Image of the demon created by my art team.

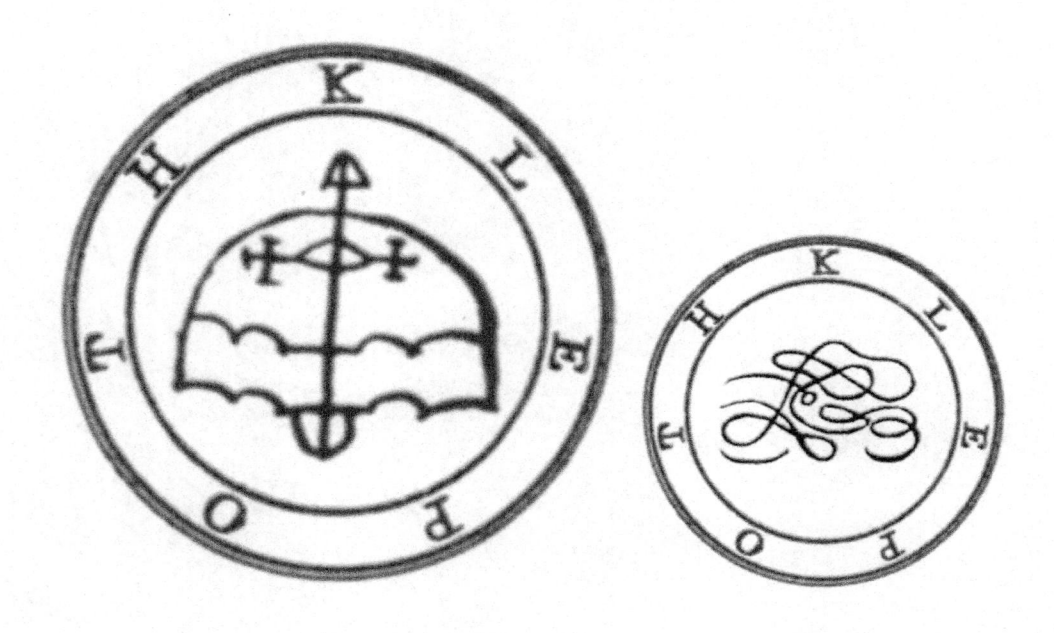

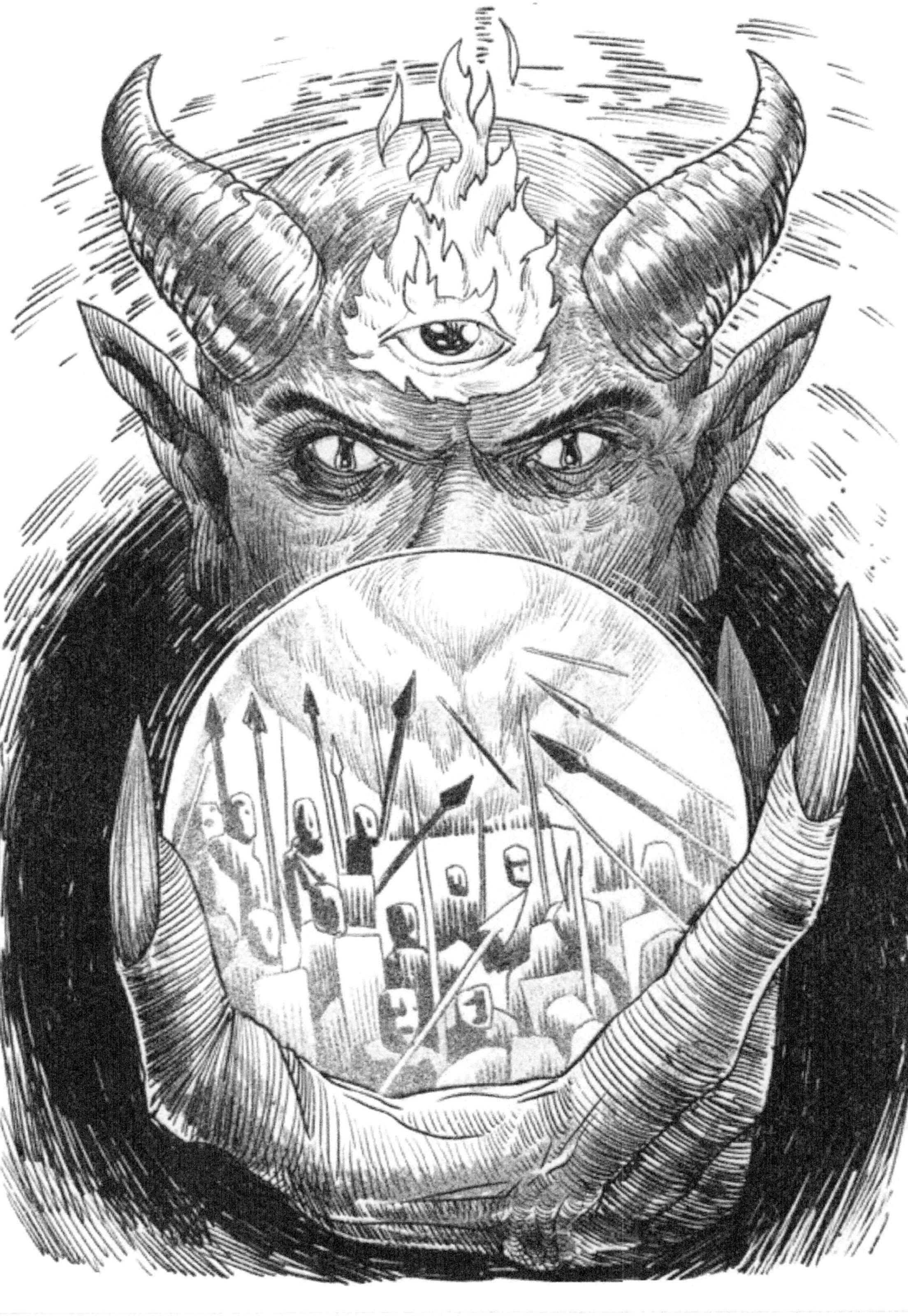

## Leraje

Leraje (or Leraie). He is a Marquis Great in Power, showing himself in the likeness of an Archer clad in Green, and carrying a Bow and Quiver. He causeth all great Battles and Contests; and maketh wounds to putrefry that are made with Arrows by Archers. This belongeth unto Sagittary. He governeth 30 Legions of Spirits, and this is his Seal, etc. -Lesser Key of Solomon. Notes: Image by my art team, sigil from the Lesser Key of Solomon.

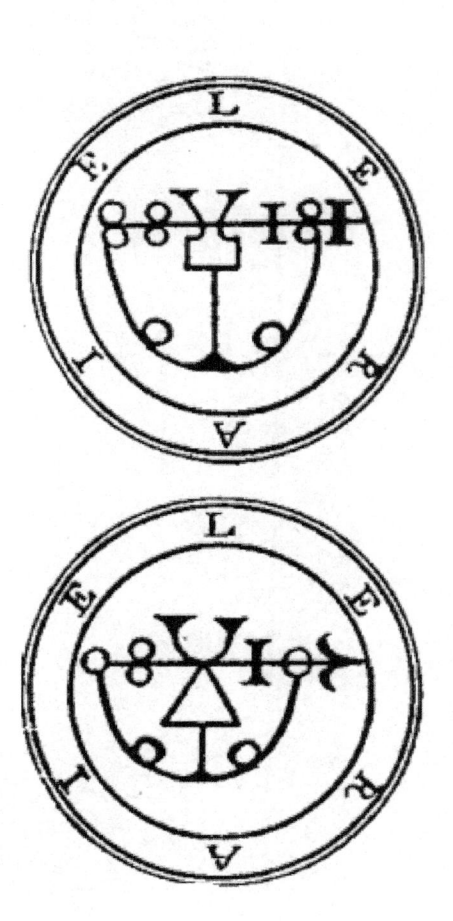

**Leviathan**

Leviathan. She is the great dragon of the sea. She is invoked in rituals to give great power to any work of magic. She has a thousand heads and knows all that has happened in the depths of the ocean. She remembers everything of our world since the beginning of time. She governs 100 legions.

Notes: Sigil from the Grimoire of Armadel.

**Lilith**

The first spirit of the moon is Lilith, the first wife of the first man. The queen of the night. Mother of harlots. The scarlet woman. The bride of Satan, or in other writings, the wife of Asmoday. She is a goddess of lust and sex. She can take thousands of forms including that of a beautiful woman whose lower body is that of a snake. She also appears as a beautiful woman with bird's feet and wings. She is to be called in the north. She has 400 legions of spirits under her command.

Notes: Sigil from an unknown source, Image by my art team.

**Lucifer**

Lucifer. He appears in the form of a handsome young boy. When he is angry his face becomes inflamed. Yet there is nothing monstrous about him. Lucifer is the link between the human and the infernal or bestial world. He is known as the light bringer. In this way he brings the light of reason and consciousness to the mind. This is also because of his ties to the planet Venus, which is sometimes the last remaining light of the heavens before the sun rises. He gives knowledge and inspiration. He is a lord of witches and of the infernal Sabbath. He can provide you with a familiar spirit. He commands 500 legions.

Notes: Sigils from the Grimorium Verum and the Grand Grimoire. Image by my art team. The Grimoire of Pope Honorius states that he should be given a mouse.

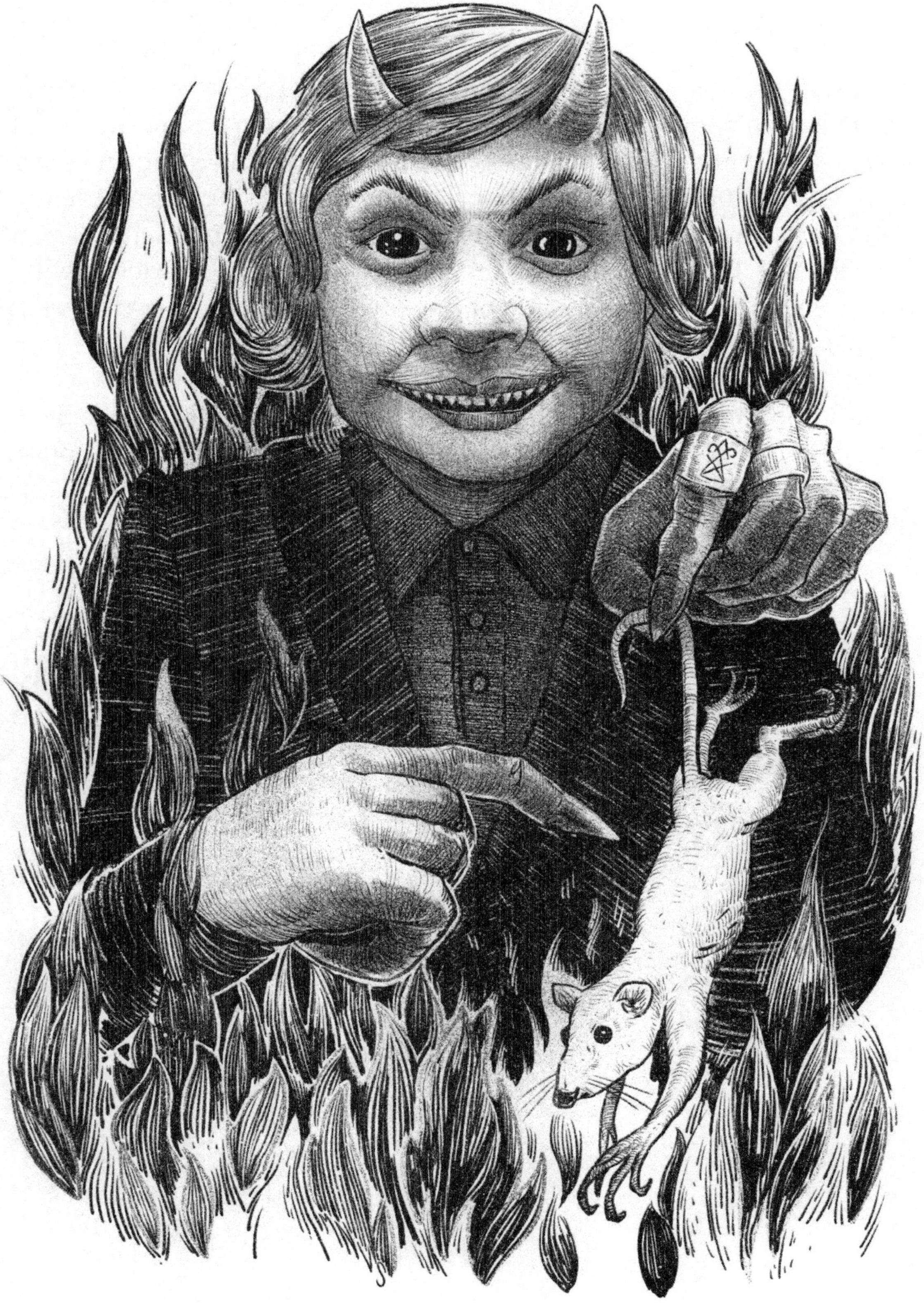

## Lucifuge Rofocale

LUCIFUGE ROFOCALE The first (of the subordinate spirits in the order of The Grand Grimoire) is the great Lucifuge Rofocale, the infernal Prime Minister who possesses the power that Lucifer gave him over all worldly riches and treasures. He has beneath him Bael, Agares and Marbas along with thousands of other demons or spirits who are his subordinates. - The Grand Grimoire. Notes: Illustration and sigil from The Grand Grimoire. This spirit is also called Tarchimache.

**Malphas**

Malphas. He appeareth at first like a Crow, but after he will put on Human Shape at the request of the Exorcist and speaks with a hoarse Voice. He is a Mighty President and Powerful. He can build Houses and High Towers and can bring to thy Knowledge Enemies' Desires and Thoughts, and that which they have done. He giveth Good Familiars. If thou makest a Sacrifice unto him he will receive it kindly and willingly, but he will deceive him that doth it. He governeth 4o Legions of Spirits, and his Seal is this, etc. -Lesser Key of Solomon

Notes: Image from the Dictionnaire Infernal, sigil from the Lesser Key of Solomon.

# Marax

Marax. He is a Great Earl and President. He appeareth like a great Bull with a Man's face. His office is to make Men very knowing in Astronomy, and all other Liberal Sciences; also he can give good Familiars, and wise, knowing the virtues of Herbs and Stones which be precious. He governeth 30 Legions of Spirits, and his Seal is this, which must be made and worn as aforesaid, etc. -Lesser Key of Solomon

Notes: Sigil from the Lesser Key of Solomon, image of the demon drawn by my art team.

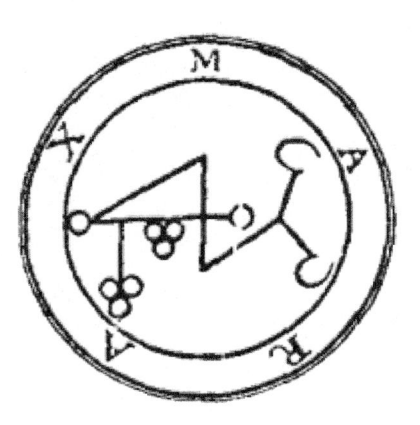

**Marbas**

Marbas. He is a Great President, and appeareth at first in the form of a Great Lion, but afterwards, at the request of the Master, he putteth on Human Shape. He answereth truly of things Hidden or Secret. He causeth Diseases and cureth them. Again, he giveth great Wisdom and Knowledge in Mechanical Arts; and can change men into other shapes. He governeth 36 Legions of Spirits. And his Seal is this, which is to be worn as aforesaid. -Lesser Key of Solomon

Notes: Sigil from the Lesser Key of Solomon, imaged of the demon drawn by my art team.

**Marchosias**

Marchosias. He is a Great and Mighty Marquis, appearing at first in the Form of a Wolf having Gryphon's Wings, and a Serpent's Tail, and Vomiting Fire out of his mouth. But after a time, at the command of the Exorcist he putteth on the Shape of a Man. And he is a strong fighter. He was of the Order of Dominations. He governeth 30 Legions of Spirits. He told his Chief, who was Solomon, that after 1,200 years he had hopes to return unto the Seventh Throne. And his Seal is this, to be made and worn as a Lamen, etc. -Lesser Key of Solomon

Notes: Image from the Dictionnaire Infernal, sigil from the Lesser Key of Solomon. Early texts describe this spirit as appearing as a she wolf. (She can teach you how to become a werewolf.)

# Mersilde

Mersilde has the power to transport anyone in an instant, anywhere. - The Grimorium Verum

Notes: "A flying goat leaping through the sky with a naked woman on its back. A link to transportation to the witches Sabbath," was the vision I received. Sigil from the Grimorium Verum, image by my art team.

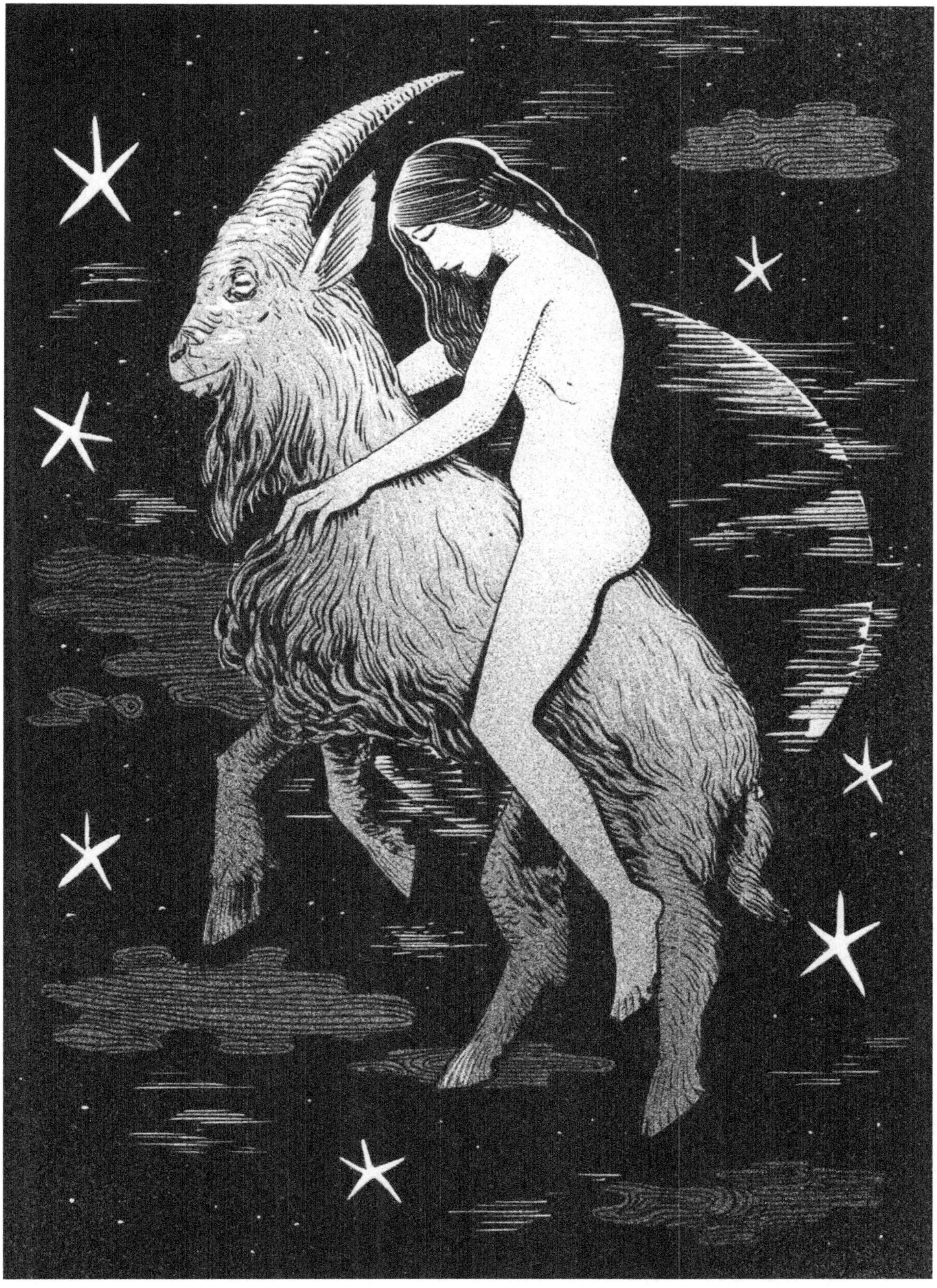

# Minoson

Minoson, is able to make anyone win at any game. – The Grimorium Verum

Notes: Sigil created by the author, represents the emotional feeling of winning. Image of the demon created by my art team. "A sort of court jester like figure."

**Morail**

Morail can make anything (or anyone) invisible. - Grimorium Verum

Notes: sigil from the Grimorium Verum. "Morail is a black cat standing on a skull from which a spider crawls from the eye, and bats fly in the sky. Dried beans fall out of the other eye. This is a nod to the skull spell for invisibility in the Grimorium Verum. What could be more invisible than a black cat, stalking in the night?" Image by my art team.

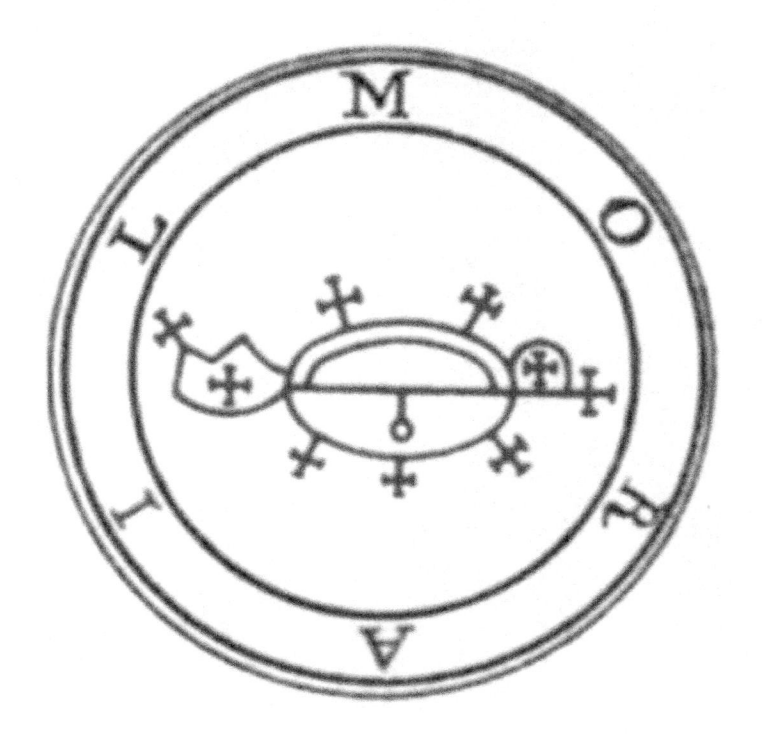

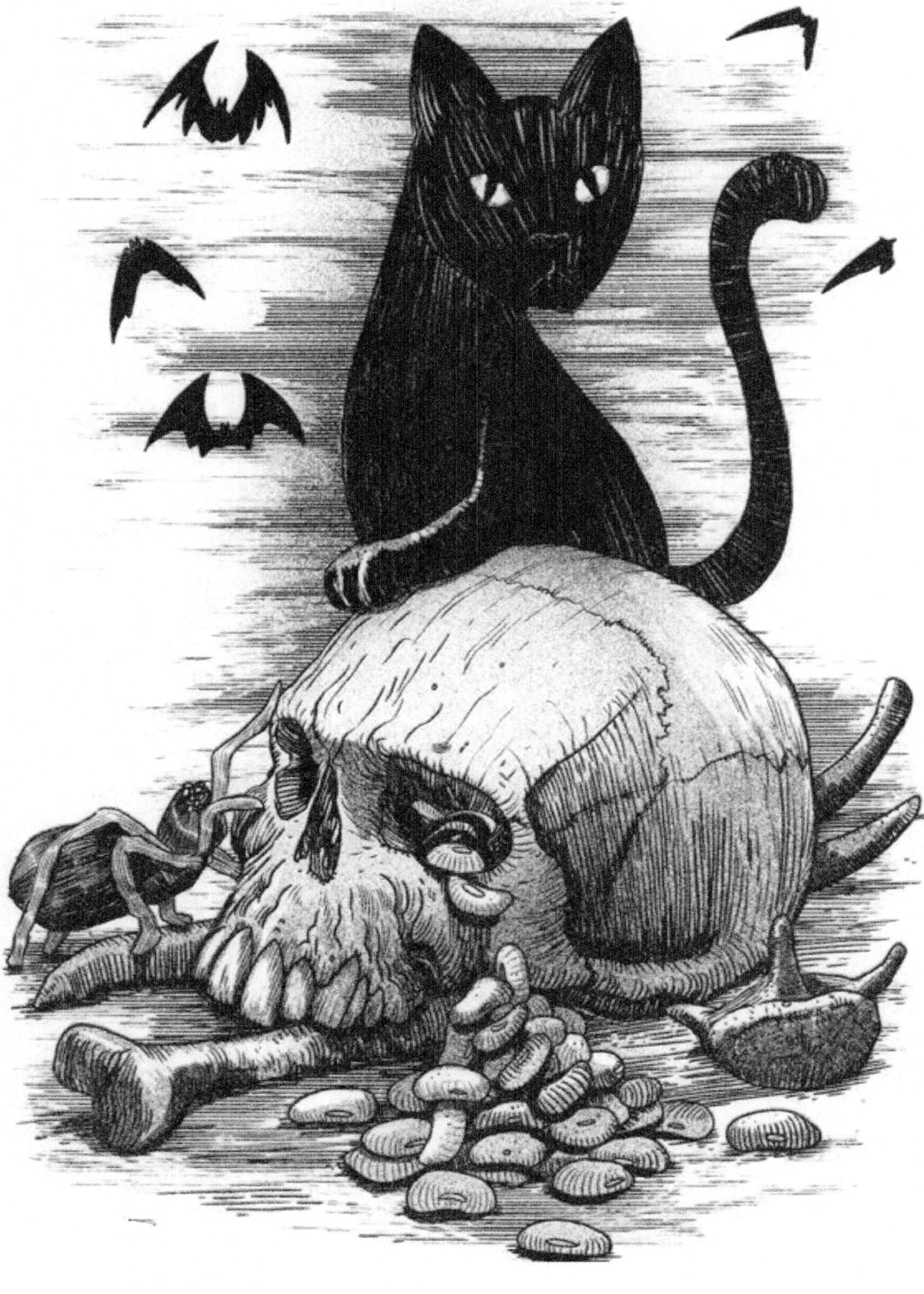

**Murmur**

Murmur, or Murmus, or Murmux. He is a Great Duke, and an Earl; and appeareth in the Form of a Warrior riding upon a Gryphon, with a Ducal Crown upon his Head. There do go before him those his Ministers with great Trumpets sounding. His Office is to teach Philosophy perfectly, and to constrain Souls Deceased to come before the Exorcist to answer those questions which he may wish to put to them, if desired. He was partly of the Order of Thrones, and partly of that of Angels. He now ruleth 30 Legions of Spirits. And his Seal is this, etc. -Lesser Key of Solomon. Notes: Image by my art team, sigil from the Lesser Key of Solomon.

**Musisin**

Musisin has power over great lords, teaches all that happens in the Republics, and the affairs of the Allies. - Grimorium Verum

Notes: Sigils from the Grimorium Verum and secrets of Solomon. "A Long bearded old man with small horns sitting on a throne staring menacingly. Many shields with coats of arms on them are at his feet to show that he is a master of making treaties and bonds between empires." Image of the demon drawn by my art team.

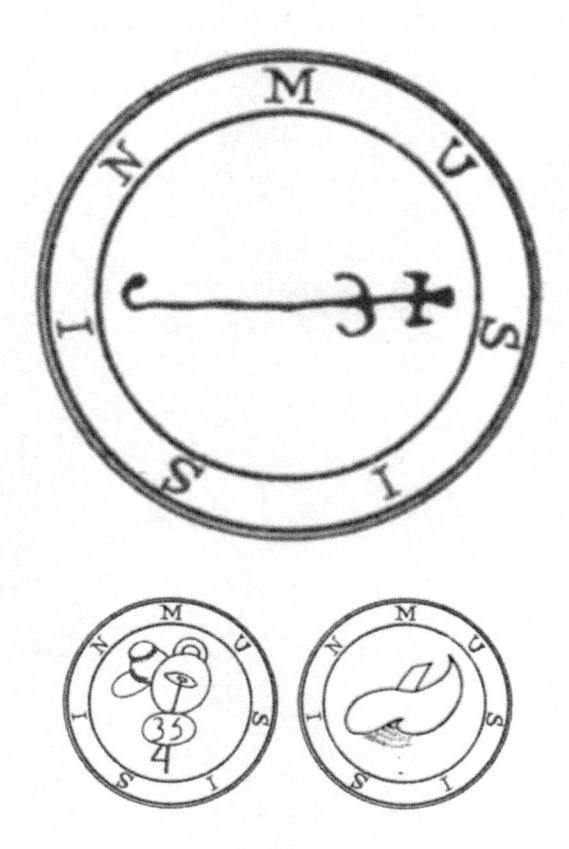

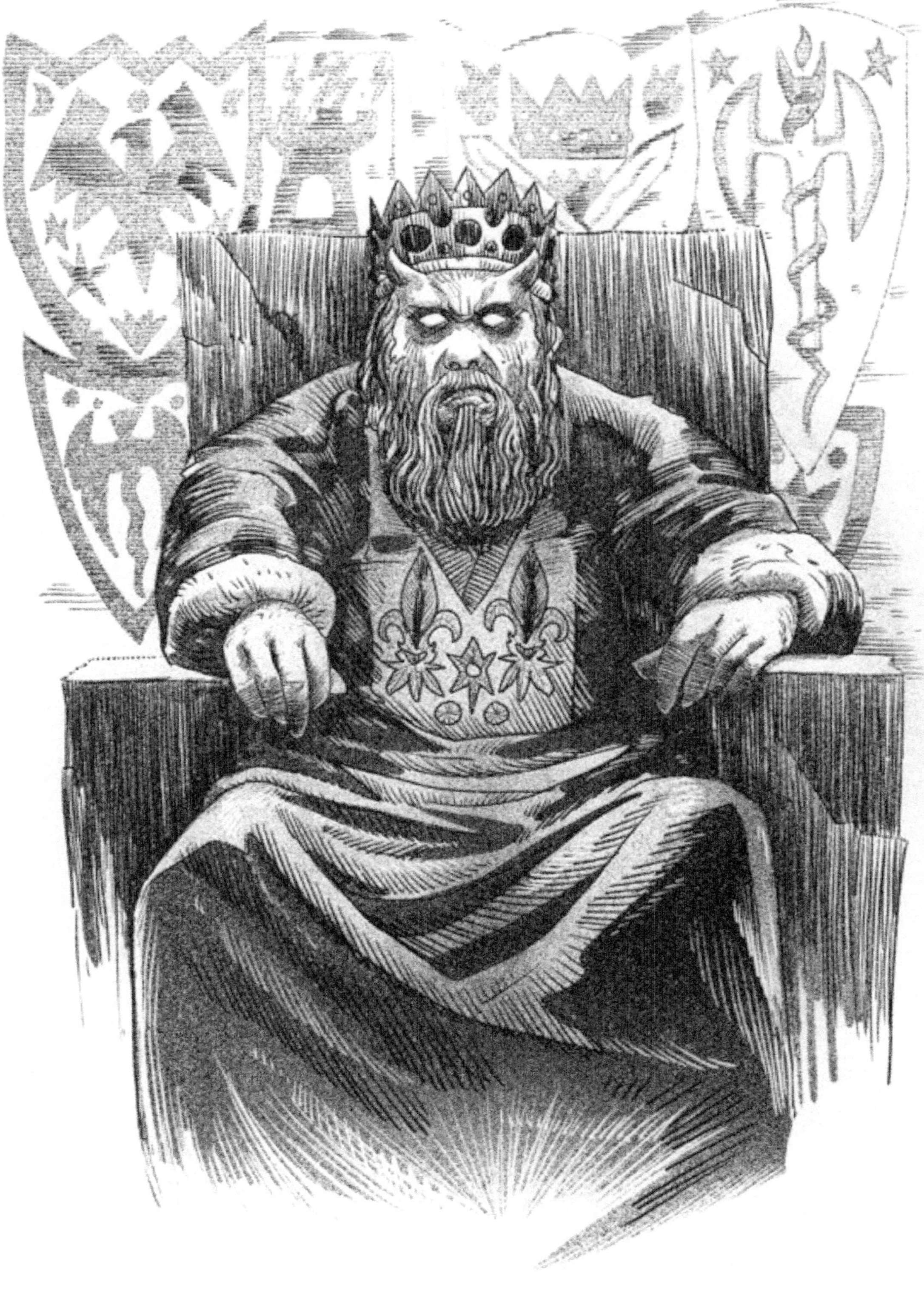

**Naberius**

Naberius. He is a most valiant Marquis, and showeth in the form of a Black Crane fluttering about the Circle, and when he speaketh it is with a hoarse voice. He maketh men cunning in all Arts and Sciences, but especially in the Art of Rhetoric. He restoreth lost Dignities and Honours. He governeth 19 Legions of Spirits. His Seal is this, which is to be worn, etc. -Lesser Key of Solomon

Notes: The image shown here is from the Dictionnaire Infernal and combines the bird description given in the Lesser Key of Solomon with the more traditional form of this spirit; the three headed dog named Cerberus. Sigil from the Lesser Key of Solomon.

**Nebiros**

Nebiros, Camp Marshal and Inspector General, who has the power to harm whoever he pleases, he can reveal the Hand of Glory, he educates on all the qualities of Metals, Minerals, Plants, and all pure & impure Animals. He also grants the art of predicting the future, being one of the greatest necromancers of all the infernal spirits. He can go anywhere and inspects all the infernal militias. He has under him Ayperos, Nuberus and Glasyabolas. - The Grand Grimoire

Notes: Sigil from The Grand Grimoire. Image of the demon drawn by my art team.

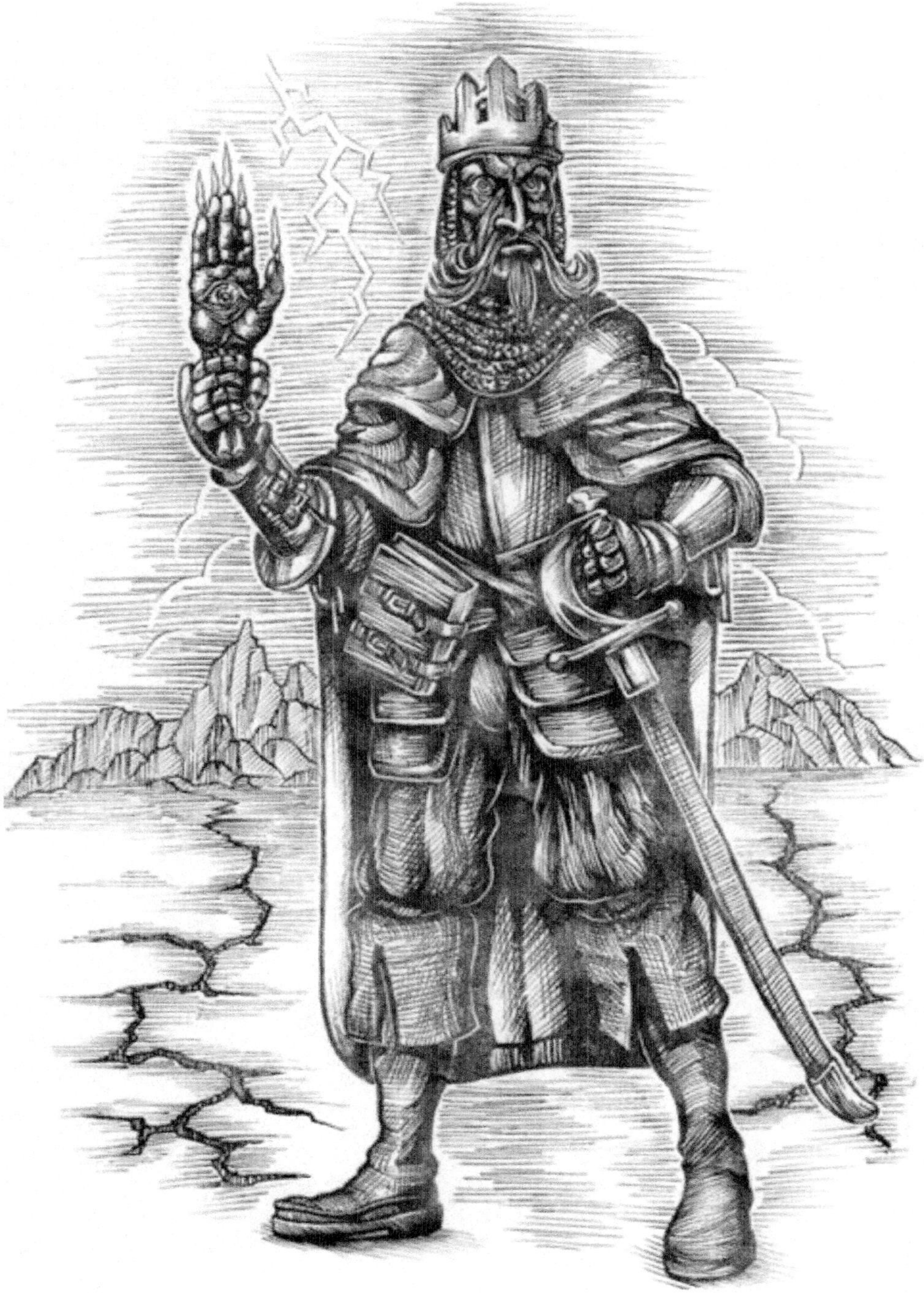

## Oriax

Oriax, or Orias. He is a Great Marquis, and appeareth in the Form of a Lion, riding upon a Horse Mighty and Strong, with a Serpent's Tail; and he holdeth in his Right Hand two Great Serpents hissing. His Office is to teach the Virtues of the Stars, and to know the Mansions of the Planets, and how to understand their Virtues. He also transformeth Men, and he giveth Dignities, Prelacies, and Confirmation thereof; also Favour with Friends and with Foes. He doth govern 30 Legions of Spirits; and his Seal is this, etc. -Lesser Key of Solomon. Notes: Image by my art team, sigil from the Lesser Key of Solomon.

**Oriens**

The spirit Oriens, King of the East. He appeareth with a fair and feminine countenance, and a goodly crown upon his head; He rideth upon an elephant, having before him numbers of musical instruments. Sometimes he appeareth in the similitude of a horse, and when he is constrained by magical incantations, assumeth a human shape. He hath under him 250 legions of inferior spirits. His power, according to the ancients, is great, and he can answer truly unto all demands, both past, present, and to come. - The Astrologer of the 19th Century

The first king raigneth in the east and is called Oriens, and he cometh in the likeness of an horse with an 100 heads or as some wright with 5 heads, but if thou call him with his company he appeareth with a fair favor and **as a woman**, riding upon an Elephant and all manner of minstrels before him, he can tell all things past, present and to come, and can prophecy truly of things to come, he can give any science earthly and earthly treasure, and he hath under him spirits innumerable of which of the best and most principal are these. - The Book of Oberon

Notes: Oriens is one of the four demon kings associated with the cardinal directions, along with Egyn (north), Amaymon (south), and Paimon (west). Oriens is associated with the direction east. Sigil from the grimoire Fasciculus Rerum Geomanticarum, image by my art team. Though called male, the spirit is clearly female.

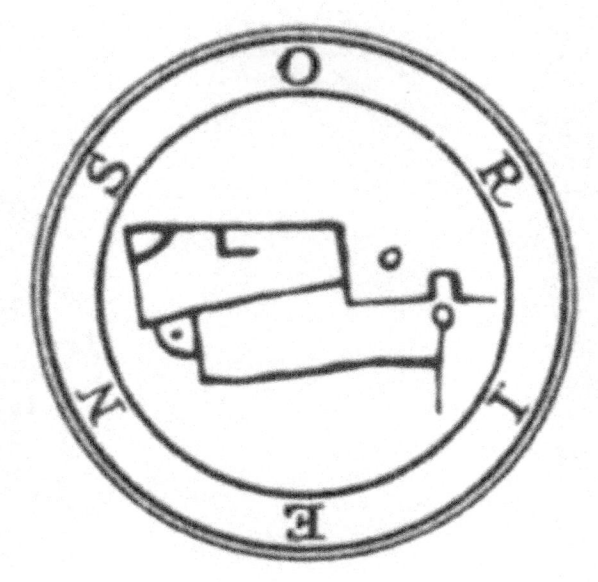

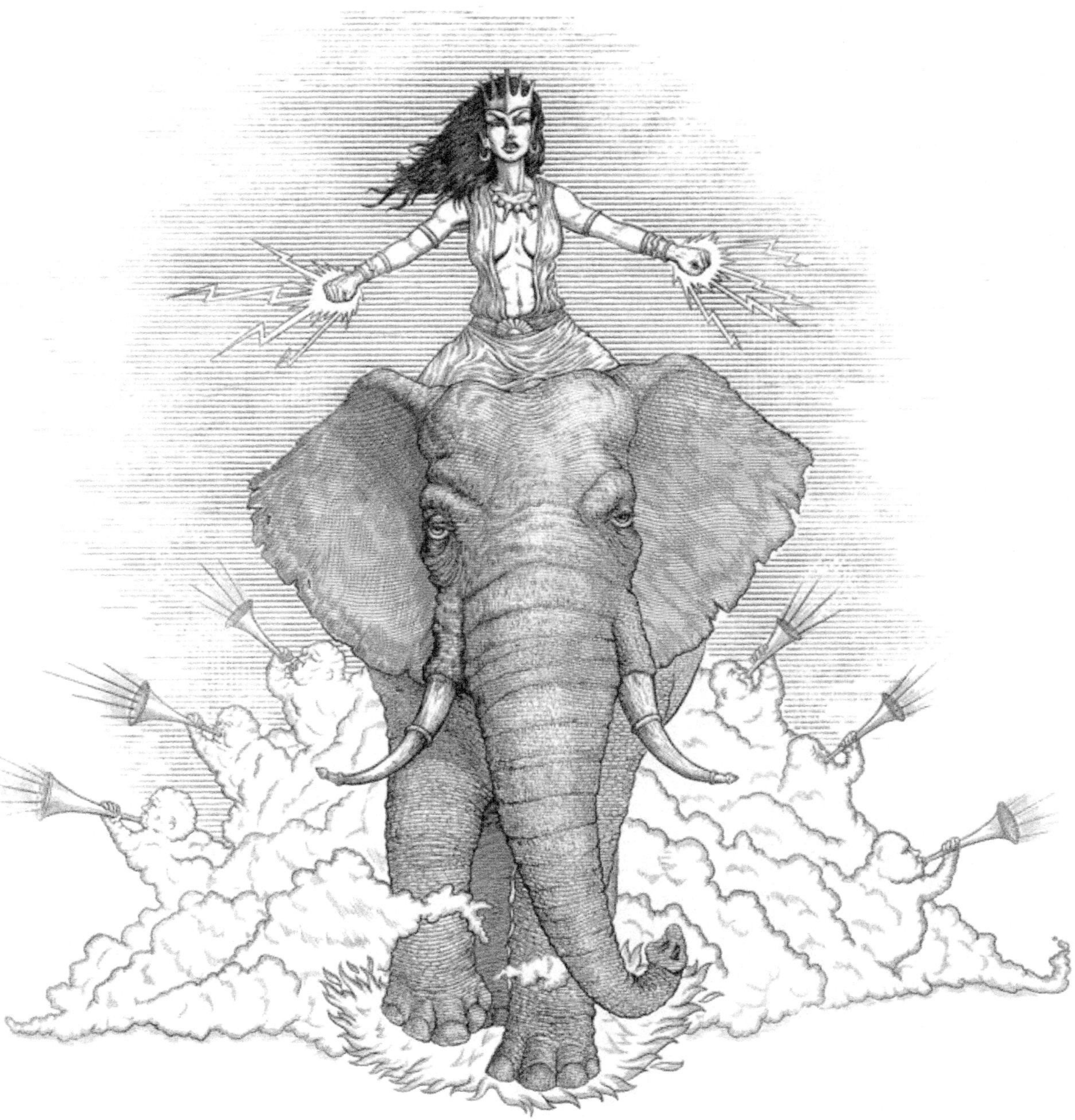

## Orobas

Orobas. He is a Great and Mighty Prince, appearing at first like a Horse; but after the command of the Exorcist he putteth on the Image of a Man. His Office is to discover all things Past, Present, and to Come; also to give Dignities, and Prelacies, and the Favour of Friends and of Foes. He giveth True Answers of Divinity, and of the Creation of the World. He is very faithful unto the Exorcist, and will not suffer him to be tempted of any Spirit. He governeth 20 Legions of Spirits. His Seal is this, etc -Lesser Key of Solomon

Notes: Image from the Dictionnaire Infernal. Sigil from the Lesser Key of Solomon.

**Ose**

Oso, Osé, or Voso. He is a Great President, and appeareth like a Leopard at the first, but after a little time he putteth on the Shape of a Man. His Office is to make one cunning in the Liberal Sciences, and to give True Answers of Divine and Secret Things; also to change a Man into any Shape that the Exorcist pleaseth, so that he that is so changed will not think any other thing than that he is in verity that Creature or Thing he is changed into. He governeth 30 Legions of Spirits, and this is his Seal, etc. -Lesser Key of Solomon. Notes: Sigil from the Lesser Key of Solomon, image by my art team.

**Paimon**

Paimon, a Great King, and very obedient unto LUCIFER. He appeareth in the form of a Man sitting upon a Dromedary with a Crown most glorious upon his head. There goeth before him also an Host of Spirits, like Men with Trumpets and well sounding Cymbals, and all other sorts of Musical Instruments. He hath a great Voice, and roareth at his first coming, and his speech is such that the Magician cannot well understand unless he can compel him. This Spirit can teach all Arts and Sciences, and other secret things. He can discover unto thee what the Earth is, and what holdeth it up in the Waters; and what Mind is, and where it is; or any other thing thou mayest desire to know. He giveth Dignity, and confirmeth the same. He bindeth or maketh any man subject unto the Magician if he so desire it. He giveth good Familiars, and such as can teach all Arts. He is to be observed towards the West. He is of the Order of Dominations. He hath under him 200 Legions of Spirits, and part of them are of the Order of Angels, and the other part of Potentates. Now if thou callest this Spirit Paimon alone, thou must make him some offering; and there will attend him two Kings called LABAL and ABALIM, and also other Spirits who be of the Order of Potentates in his Host, and 25 Legions. And those Spirits which be subject unto them are not always with them unless the Magician do compel them. His Character is this which must be worn as a Lamen before thee, etc. -Lesser Key of Solomon. Notes: Sigils from the Fasciculus Rerum Geomanticarum and lesser Key of Solomon, image by my art team.

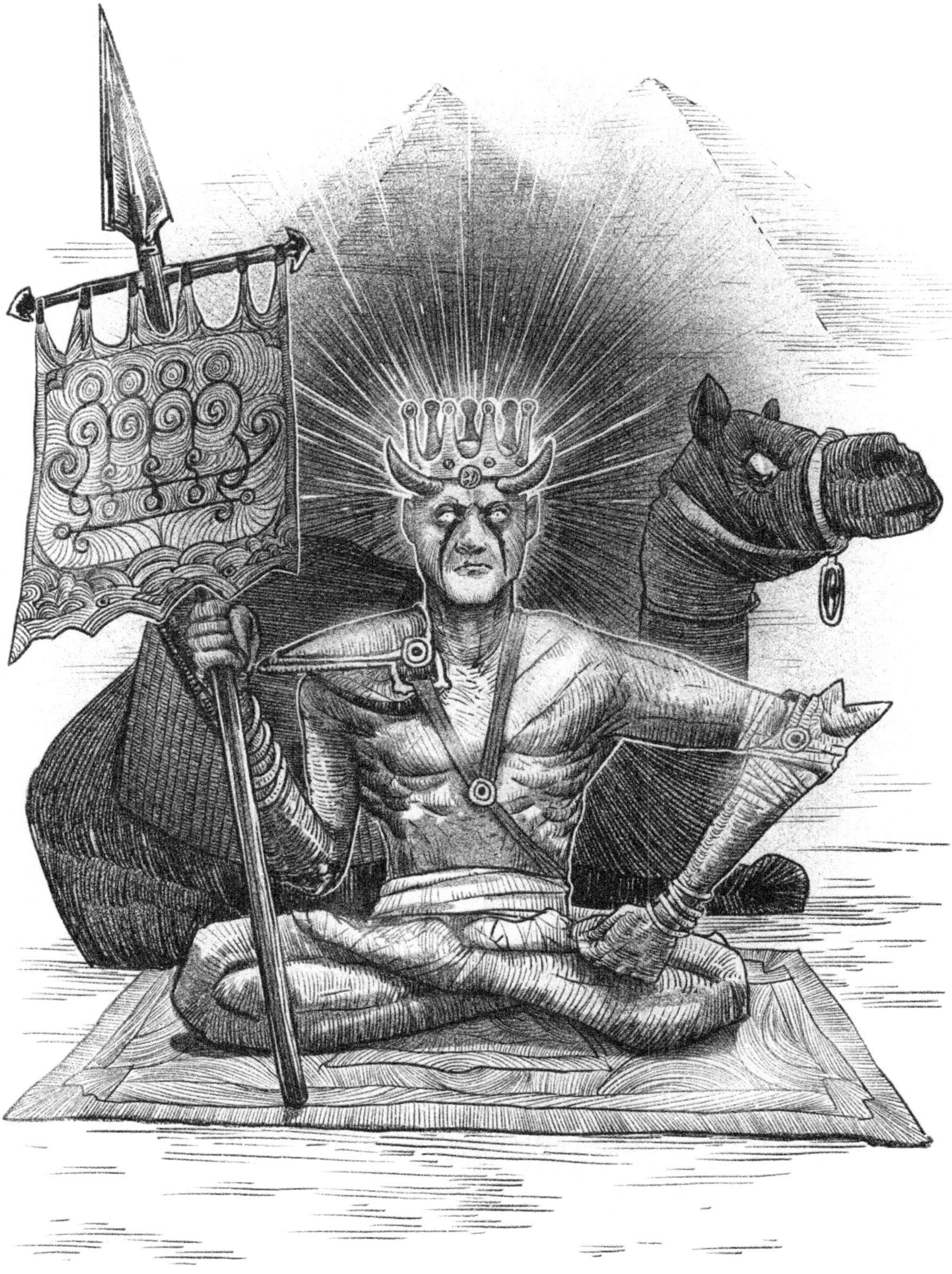

## Pentagnony

Pentagnony, or Pentagony who gives the two benefits of attaining invisibility and the love of great lords. - The Grimorium Verum

Notes: Sigil created by the author, the union of the symbol of Saturn, invisibility, and Jupiter, the love of great lords. Image of the demon created by my art team.

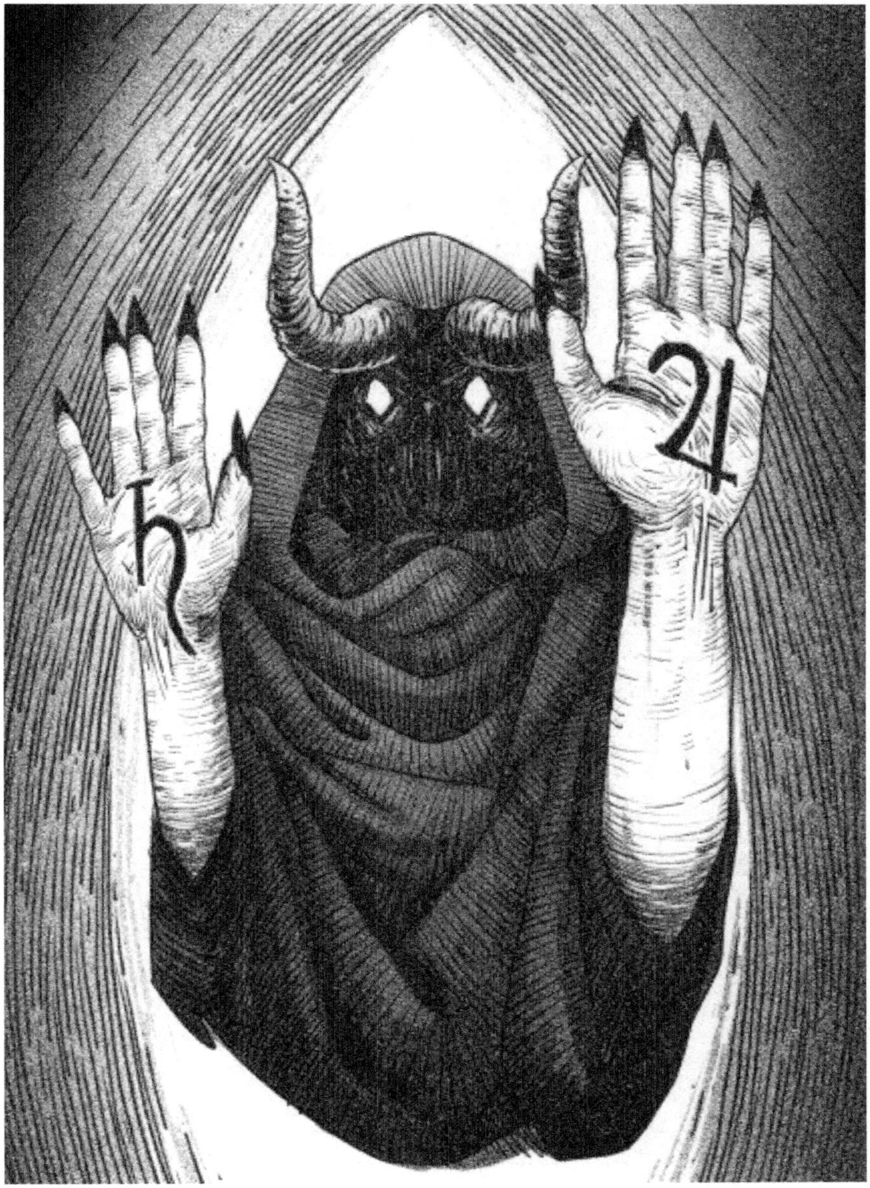

**Phenex**

Phenex (or Pheynix). He is a Great Marquis, and appeareth like the Bird Phoenix, having the Voice of a Child. He singeth many sweet notes before the Exorcist, which he must not regard, but by-and-by he must bid him put on Human Shape. Then will he speak marvellously of all wonderful Sciences if required. He is a Poet, good and excellent. And he will be willing to perform thy requests. He hath hopes also to return to the Seventh Throne after 1,200 years more, as he said unto Solomon. He governeth 20 Legions of Spirits. And his Seal is this, which wear thou, etc.- Lesser Key of Solomon

Notes: Image by my art team, sigil from the Lesser Key of Solomon.

**Proculo**

Proculo, who can cause a person to sleep for forty-eight hours, with the knowledge of the spheres of sleep. - Grimorium Verum

Notes: This sigil was created by me and represents a soul (the circle at the top) coming loose from the body (represented by the cross-like figure at the bottom) thus, to wander in the dream world. "A person lying in bed asleep in a darkened room with a bat winged demon standing over beside the bed looking down on them, wings outstretched." Illustration by my art team.

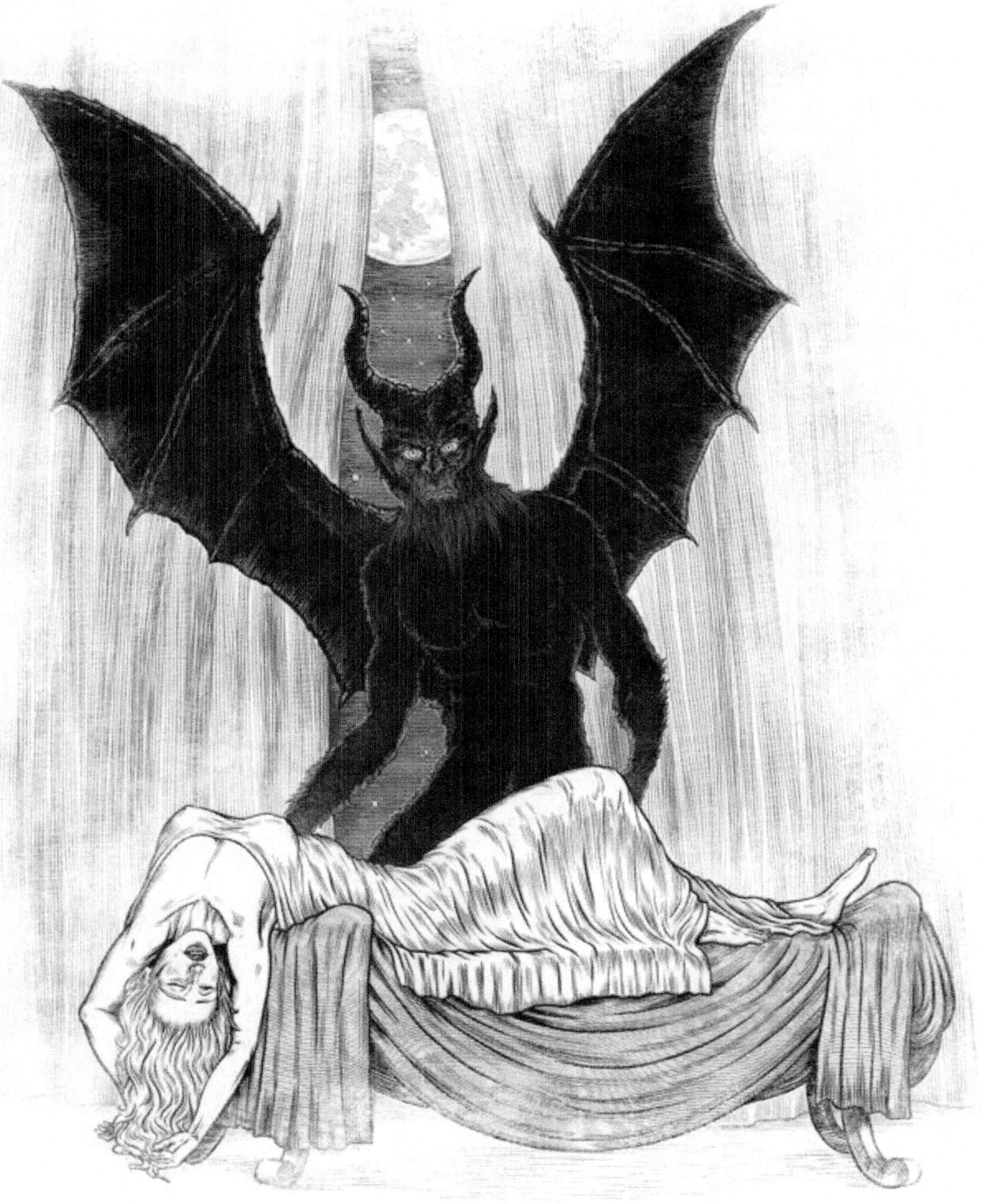

## Pruflas

Pruflas, otherwise found as Bufas, is a great prince and duke, whose abode is around the Tower of Babylon, and there he is seen like a flame outside. His head however is like that of a great night hawk. He is the author and promoter of discord, war, quarrels, and falsehood. He may not be admitted into every place. He responds generously to your requests. Under him are twenty-six legions, partly of the order of Thrones, and partly of the order of Angels.

Notes: Text from the Pseudomonarchia Daemonum, sigil created by Frater V.I.M., image by my art team.

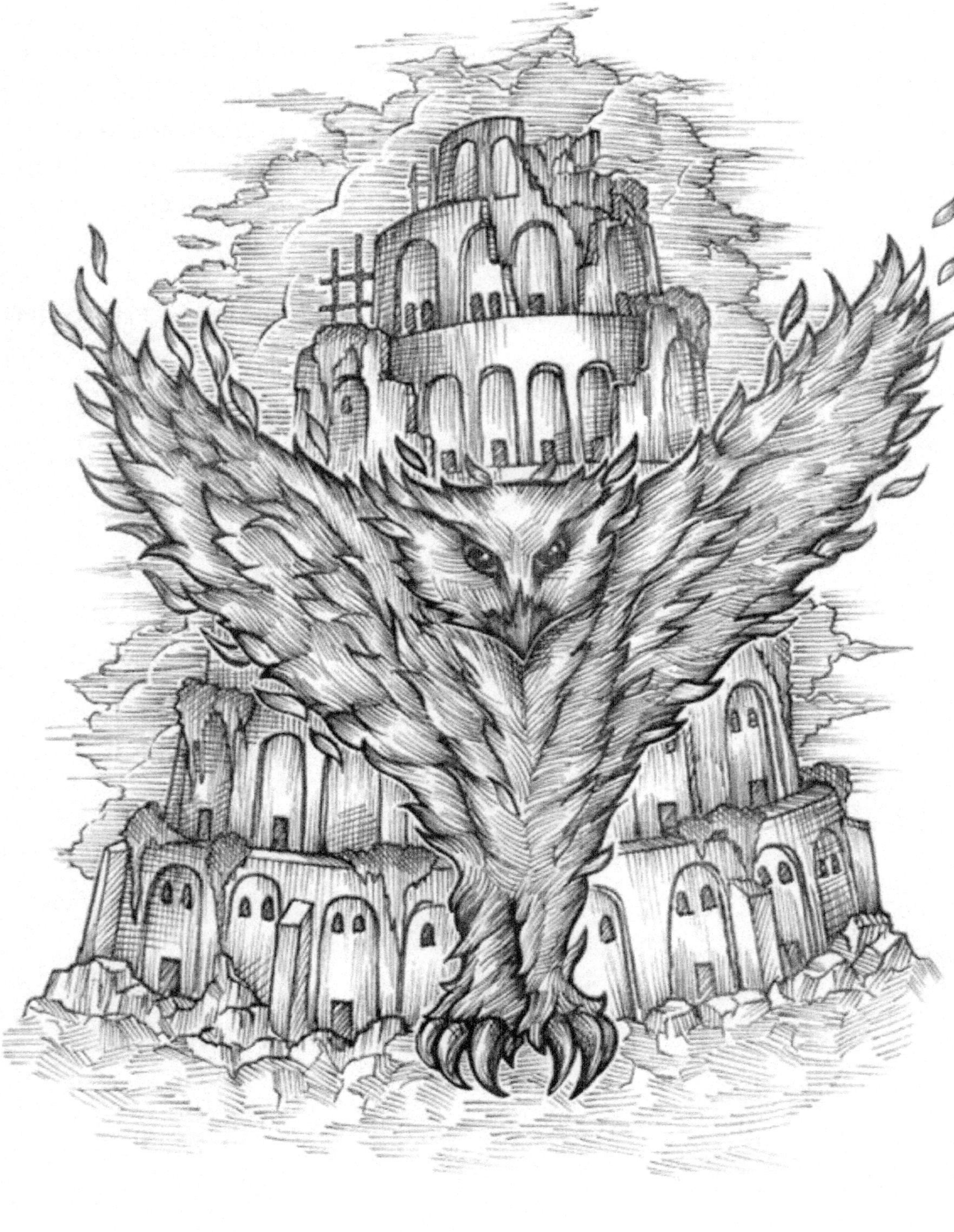

**Purson**

Purson, a Great King. His appearing is comely, like a Man with a Lion's face, carrying a cruel Viper in his hand, and riding upon a Bear. Going before him are many Trumpets sounding. He knoweth all things hidden, and can discover Treasure, and tell all things Past, Present, and to Come. He can take a Body either Human or Aërial, and answereth truly of all Earthly things both Secret and Divine, and of the Creation of the World. He bringeth forth good Familiars, and under his Government there be 22 Legions of Spirits, partly of the Order of Virtues and partly of the Order of Thrones. His Mark, Seal, or Character is this, unto the which he oweth obedience, and which thou shalt wear in time of action, etc. -Lesser Key of Solomon

Notes: Image from the Dictionnaire Infernal, sigil from the Lesser Key of Solomon.

**Raum**

Räum. He is a Great Earl; and appeareth at first in the Form of a Crow, but after the Command of the Exorcist he putteth on Human Shape. His office is to steal Treasures out King's Houses, and to carry it whither he is commanded, and to destroy Cities and Dignities of Men, and to tell all things, Past, and what Is, and what Will Be; and to cause Love between Friends and Foes. He was of the Order of Thrones. He governeth 30 Legions of Spirits; and his Seal is this, which wear thou as aforesaid. -Lesser Key of Solomon

Notes: A public domain image of a crow, sigil from the Lesser Key of Solomon.

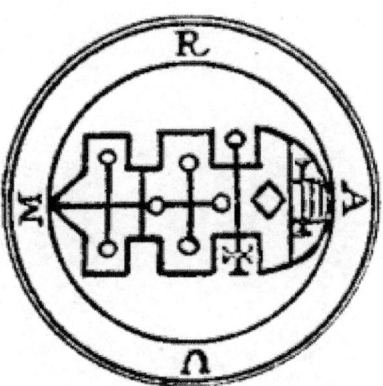

**Ronove**

Ronové. He appeareth in the Form of a Monster. He teacheth the Art of Rhetoric very well, and giveth Good Servants, Knowledge of Tongues, and Favours with Friends or Foes. He is a Marquis and Great Earl; and there be under his command 19 Legions of Spirits. His Seal is this, etc. -Lesser Key of Solomon

Notes: Image from the Dictionnaire Infernal, sigil from the Lesser Key of Solomon.

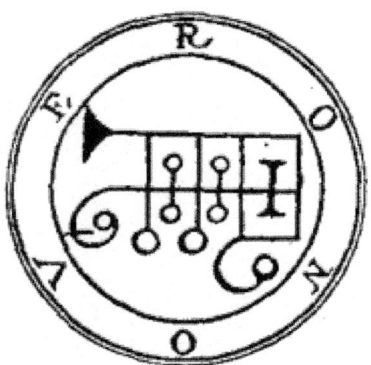

**Sabnock**

Sabnock, or Savnok. He is a Marquis, Mighty, Great and Strong, appearing in the Form of an Armed Soldier with a Lion's Head, riding on a pale-coloured horse. His office is to build high Towers, Castles, and Cities, and to furnish them with Armour, etc. Also, he can afflict Men for many days with Wounds and with Sores rotten and full of Worms. He giveth Good Familiars at the request of the Exorcist. He commandeth 50 Legions of Spirits; and his Seal is this, etc. -Lesser Key of Solomon. Notes: Image by my art team, sigil from the Lesser Key of Solomon.

**Sallos**

Sallos (or Saleos). He is a Great and Mighty Duke, and appeareth in the form of a gallant Soldier riding on a Crocodile, with a Ducal Crown on his head, but peaceably. He causeth the Love of Women to Men, and of Men to Women; and governeth 30 Legions of Spirits. His Seal is this, etc. -Lesser Key of Solomon

Notes: Image from the Dictionnaire Infernal, sigil from the Lesser Key of Solomon.

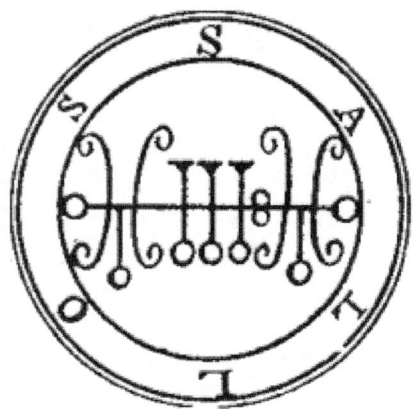

## Samigina

Samigina, a Great Marquis. He appeareth in the form of a little Horse or Ass, and then into Human shape doth he change himself at the request of the Master. He speaketh with a hoarse voice. He ruleth over 30 Legions of Inferiors. He teaches all Liberal Sciences, and giveth account of Dead Souls that died in sin. And his Seal is this, which is to be worn before the Magician when he is Invocator, etc. -Lesser Key of Solomon

Notes: Public domain image of a horse. Sigil from the Lesser Key of Solomon.

**Sargatanas**

Brigadier Sargatanas, who has the power to make one invisible, to transport one anywhere, to open all locks, to grant one the power to see whatever is happening inside homes, to teach all the tricks and subtleties of the Shepherds. He controls several brigades of spirits. He has under him Loray, Valefar and Farau. - The Grand Grimoire

Notes: Sigil from The Grand Grimoire, image created by my art team.

144 | Page

## Satanachia

SATANACHIA. Under Satanachia or Sataniciae are forty-five, or, according to other versions, fifty-four, daemons. Four of these, the chiefs, are Sergutthy, Heramael, Trimasael and Sustugriel. The others are of no great consequence. - Grimorium Verum

Satanachia. He has power over women and girls. He also has the power to make a person young or old. - The Grand Grimoire.

Notes: Is this Satanachia the same as Satan? I cannot say for sure, but I would point out that both Satan and Lucifer appear as separate spirits in the Book of Abramelin, Book of Oberon, and other grimoires. I feel strongly that this spirit is associated with the Kundalini energy.

**Scirlin**

This Invocation is to be made on virgin parchment, with the characters of the Demon (you wish to call) upon it, which causes the intermediary Scirlin to come. For from this depend all the others, and it can constrain them to appear in spite of themselves, as he has the power of the Emperor. - The Grimorium Verum

Notes: Sigil by the author. Image by my art team. Scirlin is a unique spirit that has the ability to go and get any other spirit. A very useful spirit indeed.

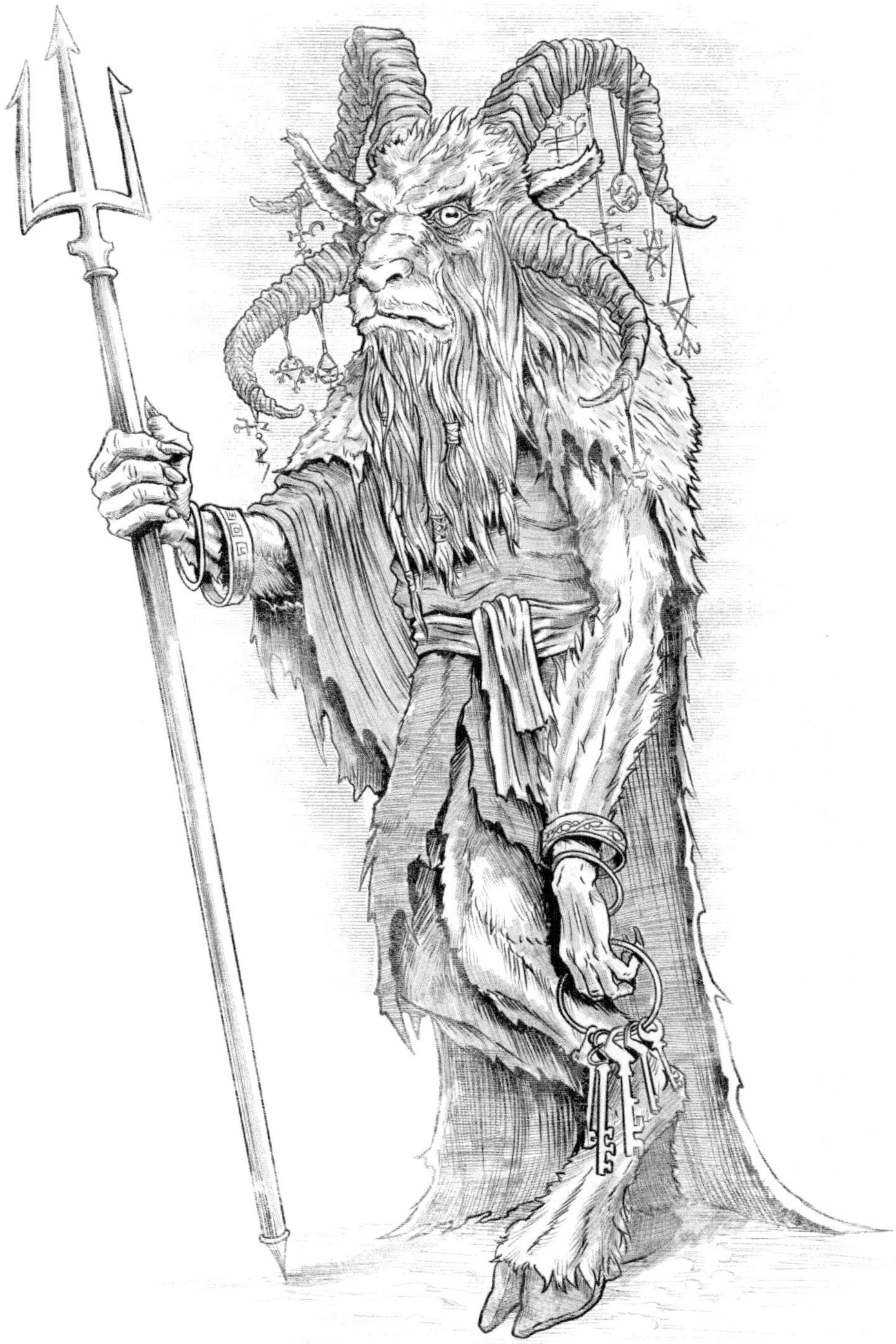

**Seere**

Seere, Sear, or Seir. He is a Mighty Prince, and Powerful, under AMAYMON, King of the East. He appeareth in the Form of a Beautiful Man, riding upon a Winged Horse. His Office is to go and come; and to bring abundance of things to pass on a sudden, and to carry or re-carry anything whither thou wouldest have it to go, or whence thou wouldest have it from. He can pass over the whole Earth in the twinkling of an Eye. He giveth a True relation of all sorts of Theft, and of Treasure hid, and of many other things. He is of an indifferent Good Nature, and is willing to do anything which the Exorcist desireth. He governeth 26 Legions of Spirits. And this his Seal is to be worn, etc. -Lesser Key of Solomon. Notes: Image by my art team, sigils from the Lesser Key of Solomon.

**Segal**

Segal will cause all sorts of prodigies to appear. - The Grimorium Verum

Notes: Prodigies is defined as omens, or spectacular events, or spectacularly talented people. A demon pointing to a comet perhaps. Sigil from the Grimorium Verum, image by my art team.

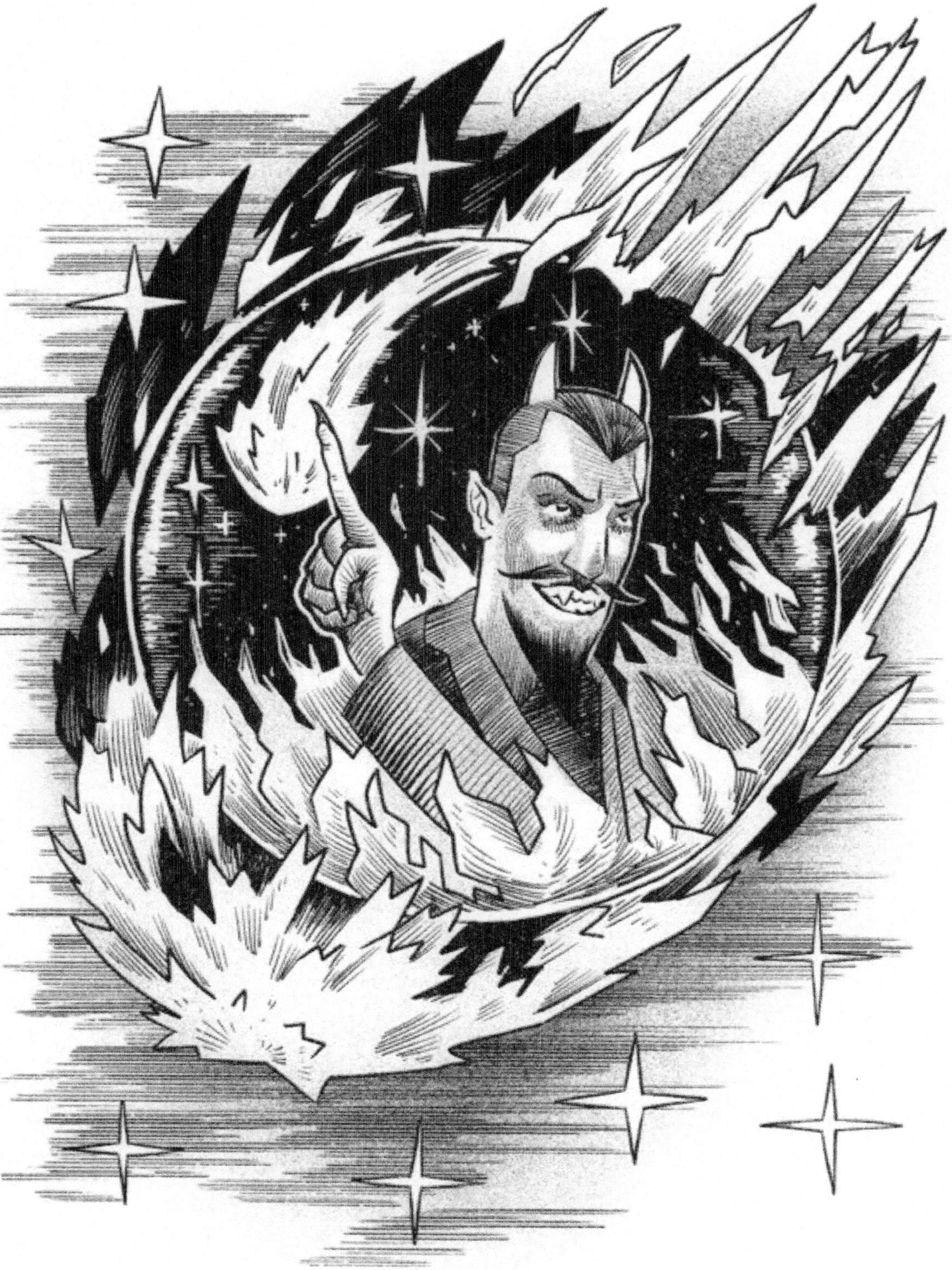

**Sergulath**

Sergulath gives every means of speculation. In addition, he instructs as to the methods of breaking the ranks and strategy of opponents. - The Grimorium Verum

Notes: "A demon playing chess. He looks like Satan with horns and bat wings, yet a lesser demon. The view is across the table from him as if the viewer is playing chess with him and it is their move, and the demon is looking at them expectantly." sigil from the Grimorium Verum, image of the demon drawn by my art team.

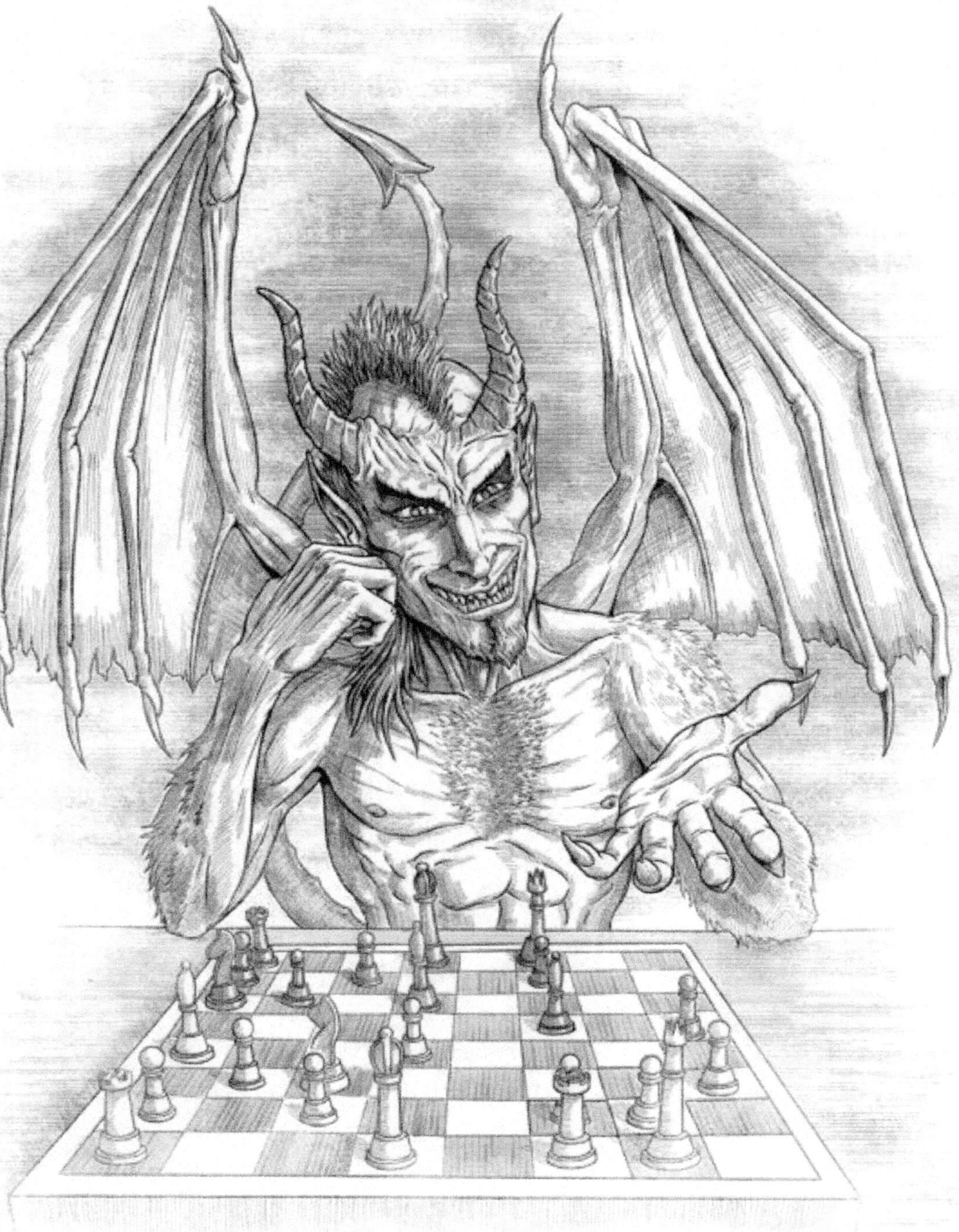

**Serguthy**

Sergutthy has power over maidens and wives when things are favorable. - Grimorium Verum

Notes: The doll that he holds symbolizes that he teaches those who learn from him, the art of binding their lovers to them with Voodoo dolls. A love/lust demon. Sigil from the Grimorium Verum, image drawn by my art team.

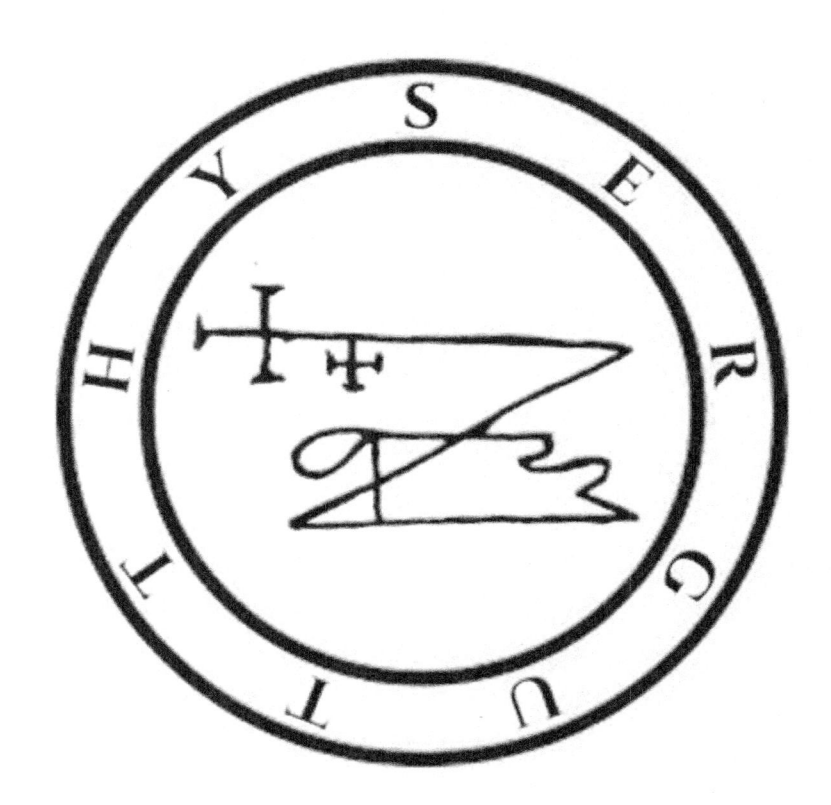

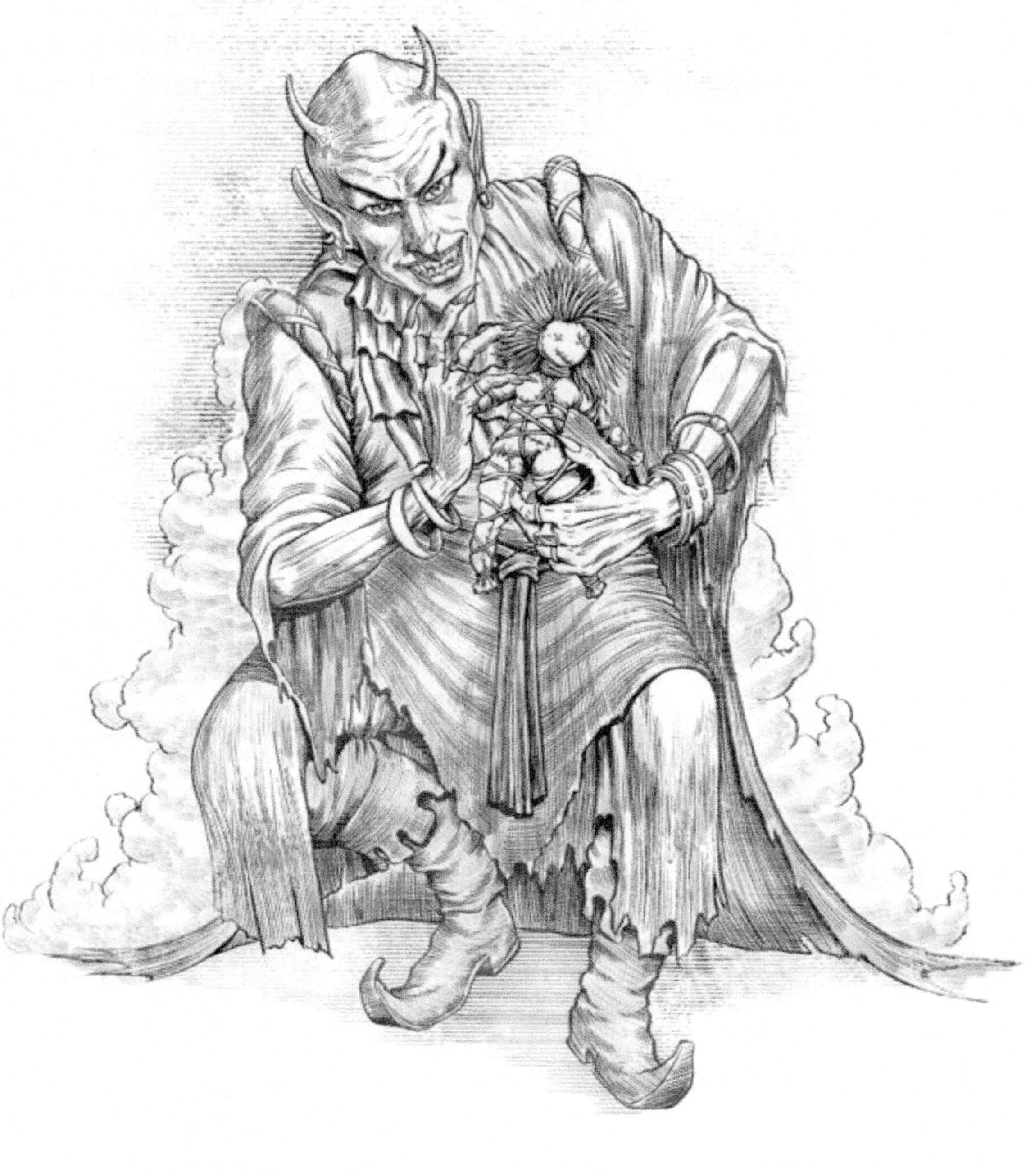

**Shax**

Shax, or Shaz (or Shass). He is a Great Marquis and appeareth in the Form of a Stock-Dove, speaking with a voice hoarse, but yet subtle. His Office is to take away the Sight, Hearing, or Understanding of any Man or Woman at the command of the Exorcist; and to steal money out of the houses of Kings, and to carry it again in 1,200 years. If commanded he will fetch Horses at the request of the Exorcist, or any other thing. But he must first be commanded into a Triangle, Δ, or else he will deceive him, and tell him many Lies. He can discover all things that are Hidden, and not kept by Wicked Spirits. He giveth good Familiars, sometimes. He governeth 30 Legions of Spirits, and his Seal is this, etc. -Lesser Key of Solomon

Notes: Image from the Dictionnaire Infernal, sigil from the Lesser Key of Solomon.

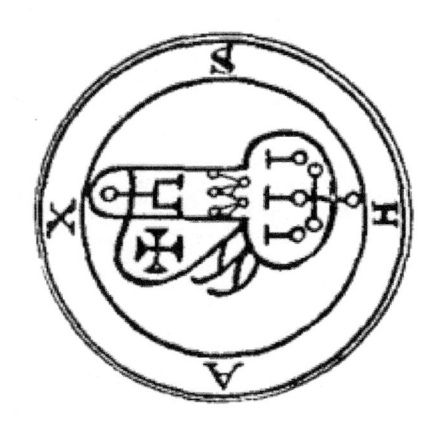

**Sidragosam**

Sidragosam, causes any girl to dance in the nude. - The True Grimoire

Notes: Sigil created by the author, the large "T" represents the demon Sidragosam, and the smaller "T" represents the dancing girl. Image created by my art team.

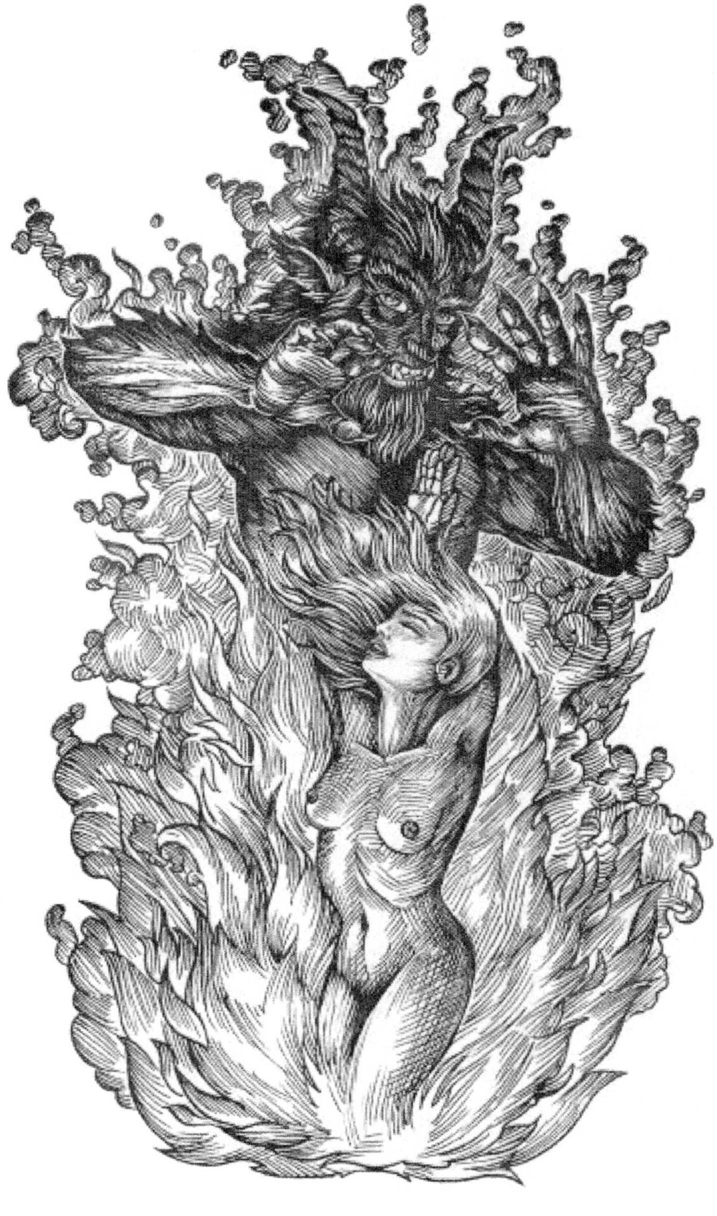

**Sirchade**

Sirchade makes you see all sorts of natural and supernatural animals. - The Grimorium Verum

Notes: The Grimoire of Honorius says that Sirchade is attributed to Thursday and that a little bread should be given to him. Sigil from the Grimorium Verum, image drawn by my art team. A supernatural animal.

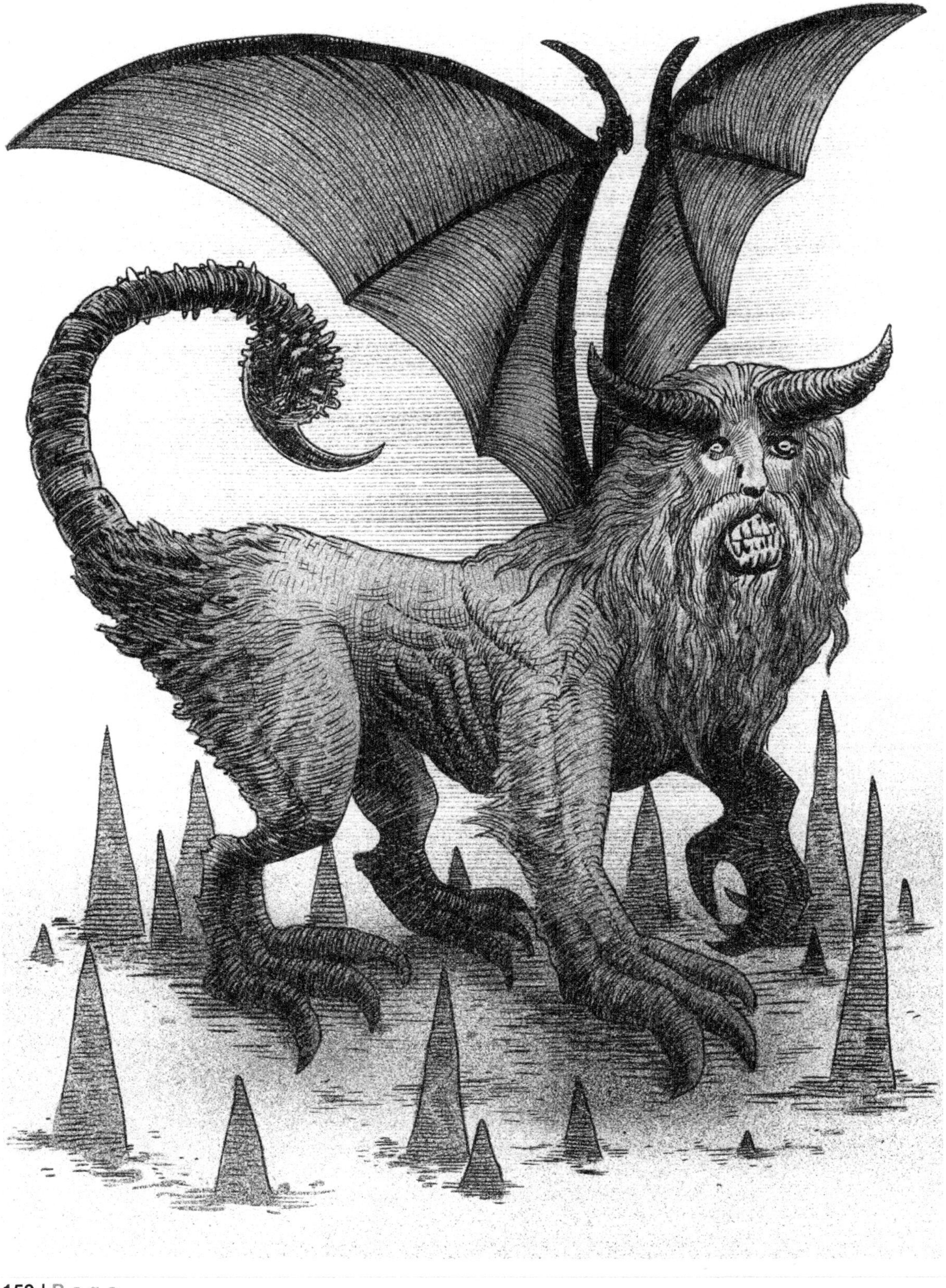

**Sitri**

Sitri. He is a Great Prince, and appeareth at first with a Leopard's head and the Wings of a Gryphon, but after the command of the Master of the Exorcism he putteth on Human shape, and that very beautiful. He enflameth men with Women's love, and Women with Men's love; and causeth them also to show themselves naked if it be desired. He governeth 60 Legions of Spirits. His Seal is this, to be worn as a Lamen before thee, etc -Lesser Key of Solomon. Notes: Image by my art team, sigil from the Lesser Key of Solomon.

**Stolas**

Stolas, or Stolos. He is a Great and Powerful Prince, appearing in the Shape of a Mighty Raven at first before the Exorcist; but after he taketh the image of a Man. He teacheth the Art of Astronomy, and the Virtues of Herbs and Precious Stones. He governeth 26 Legions of Spirits; and his Seal is this, which is, etc. -Lesser Key of Solomon

Notes: Image from the Dictionnaire Infernal, sigil from the Lesser Key of Solomon.

**Surgat**

Surgat opens every kind of lock. - Grimorium Verum

Notes: The Grimoire of Honorius says that he should be invoked on a Sunday, and offered the hair of a fox, even though he demands a hair of your head. It also states that his office is to discover and transport all treasures and perform anything that you wish. Image drawn in the form of a fox by my art team, sigil from the Grimorium Verum.

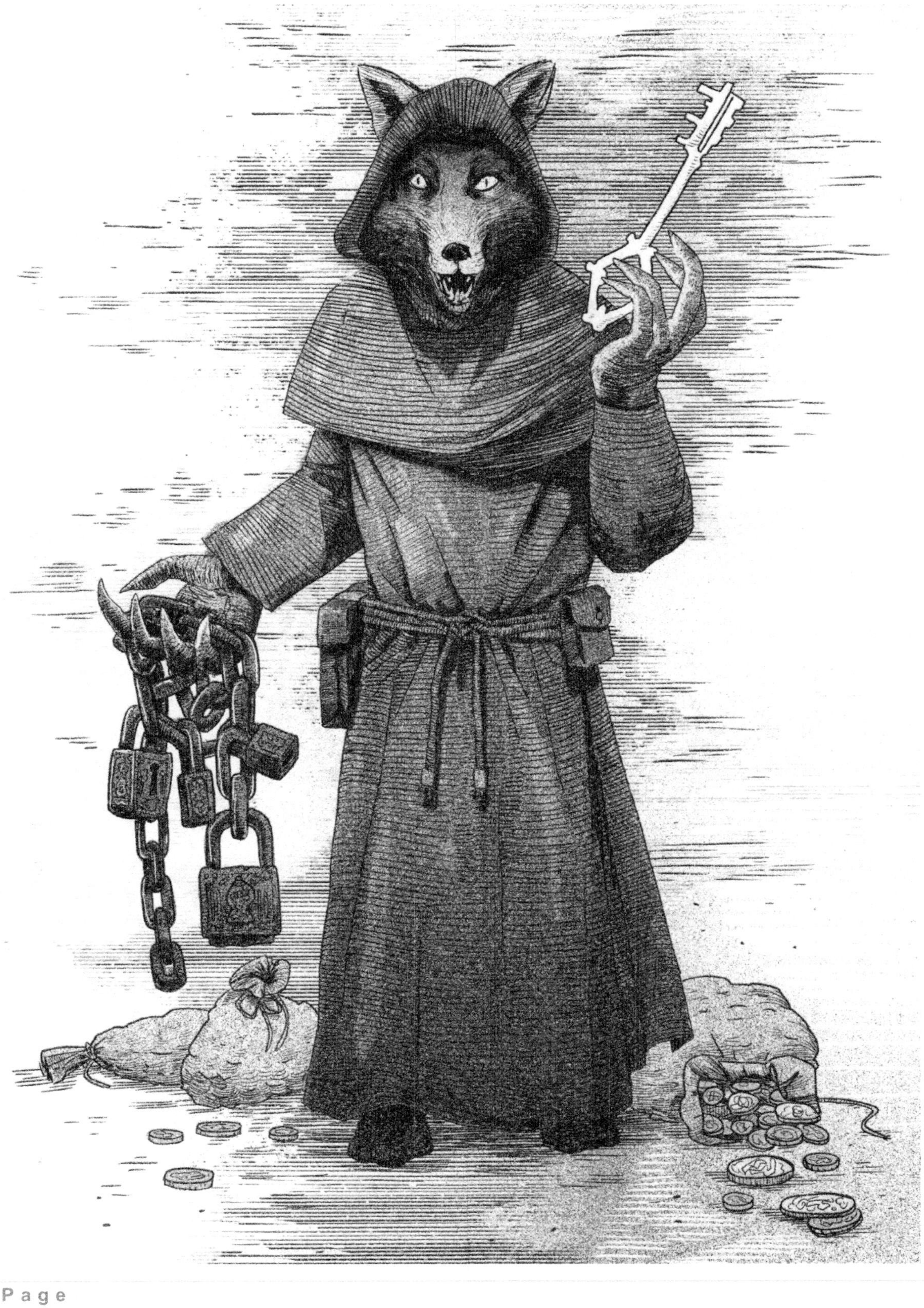

**Sustugriel**

Sustugriel teaches the art of magic. He gives familiar spirits that can be used for all purposes, and he also gives mandragores. - Grimorium Verum

Notes: Sigil from the Grimorium Verum, image of the demon drawn by my art team.

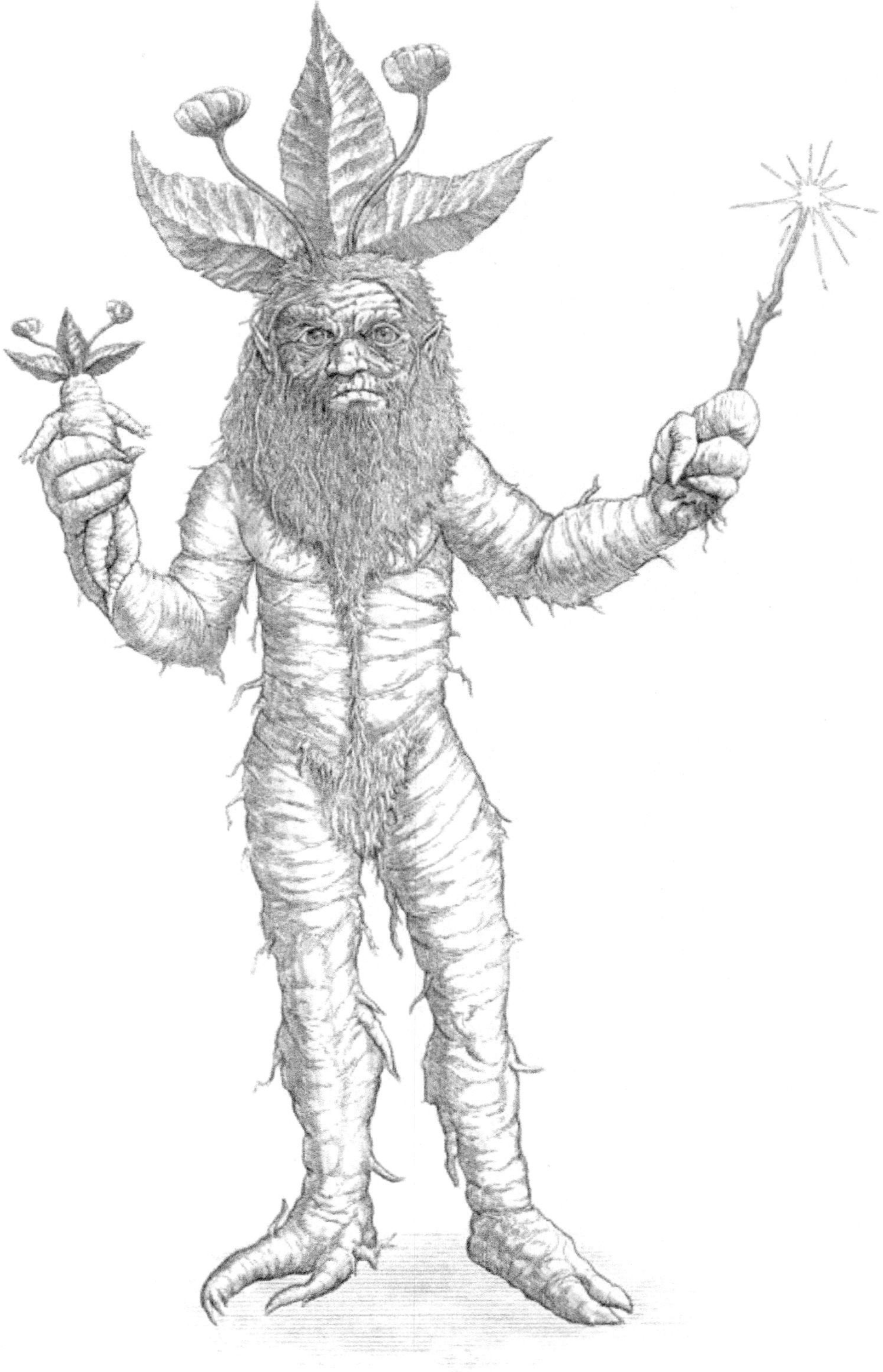

## Syrach

SYRACH There are yet other daemons, apart from these, who are under Duke Syrach. There are eighteen of these, and their names are: I. Clauneck II. Musisin III. Bechaud IV. Frimost V. Klepoth VI. Khil VII. Mersilde VIII. Clisthert IX. Sirchade X. Segal XI. Hicpacth XII. Humots XIII. Frucissiere XIV. Guland XV. Surgat XVI. Morail XVII. Frutimiere XVIII. Huictiigaras. Notes: All we know of Duke Syrach is that he is a mighty General who commands the 18 mighty spirits under him. Sigil from the Secrets of Solomon. Image of the demon drawn drawn by my art team.

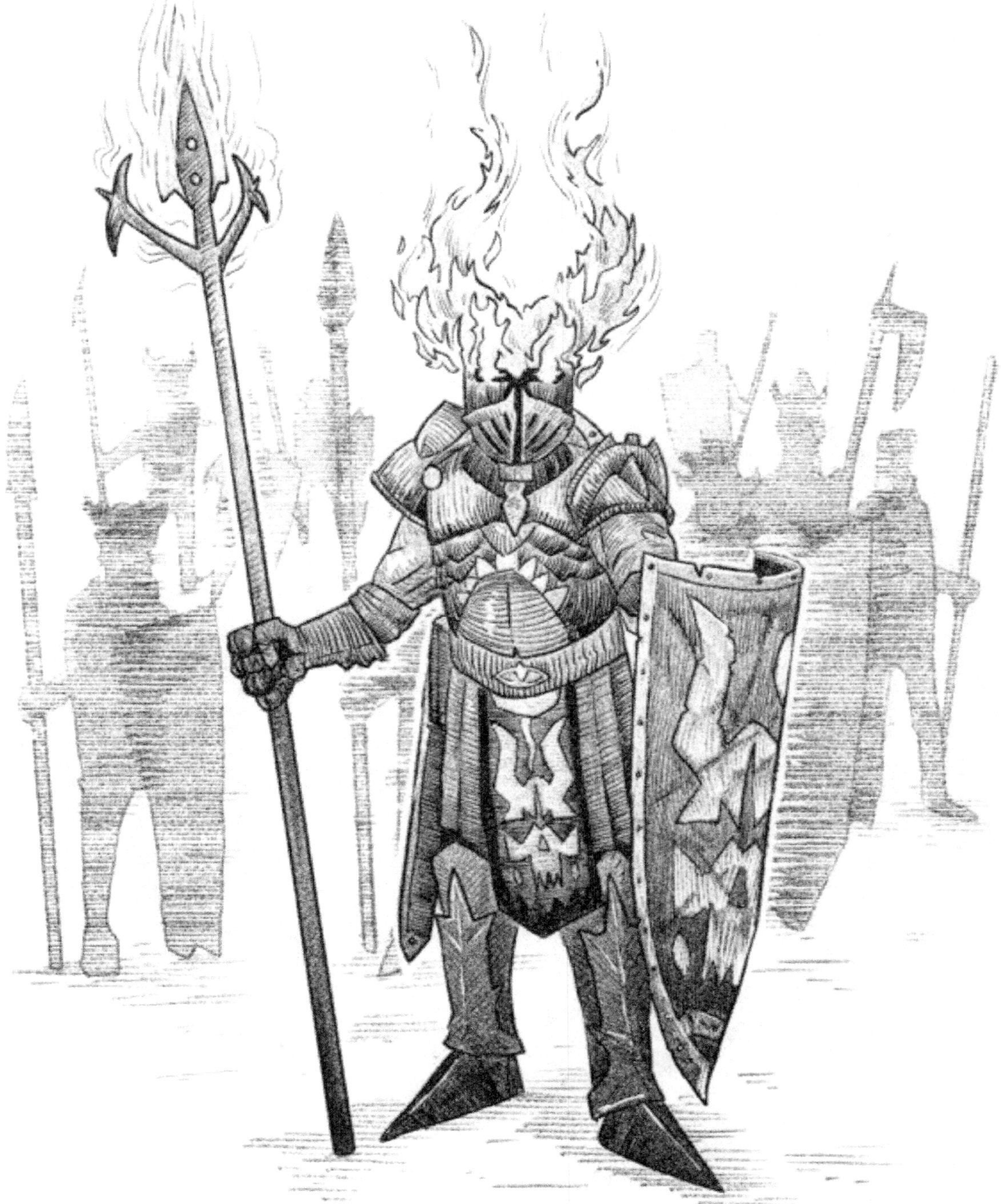

**Trimasael**

Trimasael teaches chemistry and all means of conjuring of the nature of deceit or sleight-of-hand. He also teaches the secret of making the Powder of Projection, by means of which the base metals may be turned into gold or silver. -Grimorium Verum

Notes: Sigil from the Grimorium Verum, image of the demon drawn by my art team.

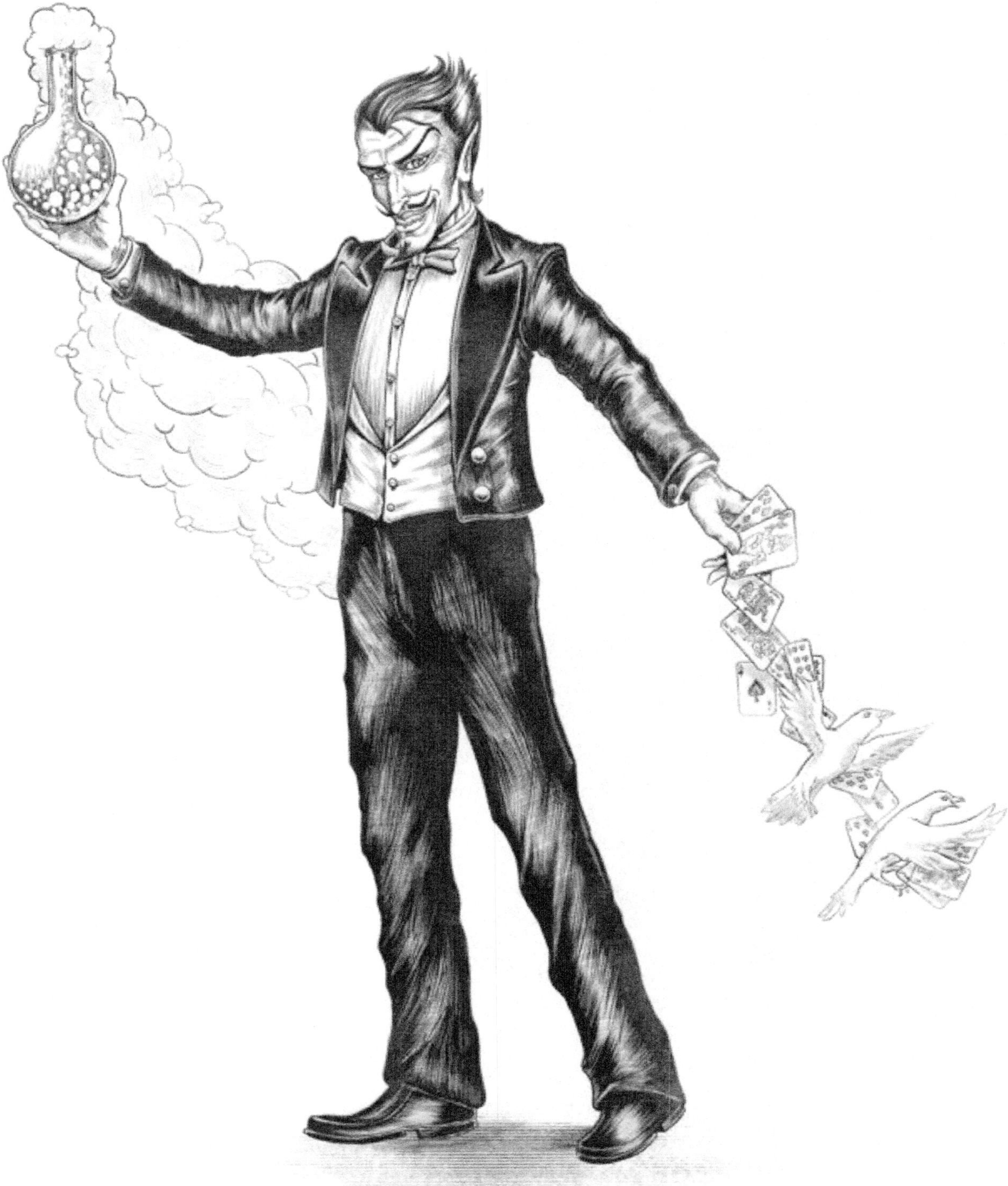

**Uvall**

Uvall, or Vual, or Voval. He is a Duke, Great, Mighty, and Strong; and appeareth in the Form of a Mighty Dromedary at the first, but after a while at the Command of the Exorcist he putteth on Human Shape, and speaketh the Egyptian Tongue, but not perfectly. His Office is to procure the Love of Women, and to tell Things Past, Present, and to Come. He also procureth Friendship between Friends and Foes. He was of the Order of Potestates or Powers. He governeth 37 Legions of Spirits, and his Seal is this, to be made and worn before thee, etc. -Lesser Key of Solomon

Notes: Image from the Dictionnaire Infernal, sigil from the Lesser Key of Solomon.

**Valak**

Volac, or Valak, or Valu. He is a President Mighty and Great, and appeareth like a Child with Angel's Wings, riding on a Two-headed Dragon. His Office is to give True Answers of Hidden Treasures, and to tell where Serpents may be seen. The which he will bring unto the Exorciser without any Force or Strength being by him employed. He governeth 38 Legions of Spirits, and his Seal is thus. -Lesser Key of Solomon

Notes: Image from the Dictionnaire Infernal, sigil from the Lesser Key of Solomon.

**Valefor**

Valefor. He is a mighty Duke, and appeareth in the shape of a Lion with an Ass's Head, bellowing. He is a good Familiar, but tempteth them he is a familiar of to steal. He governeth 10 Legions of Spirits. His Seal is this, which is to be worn, whether thou wilt have him for a Familiar, or not. -Lesser Key of Solomon.

Notes: Image crested by my art team, sigil from the Lesser Key of Solomon.

## Vapula

Vapula, or Naphula. He is a Duke Great, Mighty, and Strong; appearing in the Form of a Lion with Gryphon's Wings. His Office is to make Men Knowing in all Handicrafts and Professions, also in Philosophy, and other Sciences. He governeth 36 Legions of Spirits, and his Seal or Character is thus made, and thou shalt wear it as aforesaid, etc. -Lesser Key of Solomon

Notes: Image by my art team, sigil from the Lesser Key of Solomon.

**Vassago**

Vassago is a Mighty Prince, being of the same nature as Agares. He is called Vassago. This Spirit is of a Good Nature, and his office is to declare things Past and to Come, and to discover all things Hid or Lost. And he governeth 26 Legions of Spirits, and this is his Seal. -Lesser Key of Solomon

Notes: Image created by my art team, sigil from the Lesser Key of Solomon.

**Vepar**

Vepar, or Vephar. He is a Duke Great and Strong, and appeareth like a Mermaid. His office is to govern the Waters, and to guide Ships laden with Arms, Armour, and Ammunition, etc., thereon. And at the request of the Exorcist he can cause the seas to be right stormy and to appear full of ships. Also he maketh men to die in Three Days by Putrefying Wounds or Sores, and causing Worms to breed in them. He governeth 29 Legions of Spirits, and his Seal is this, etc.  -Lesser Key of Solomon. Notes: Image created by my art team, sigil from the Lesser Key of Solomon.

**Vine**

Viné, or Vinea. He is a Great King, and an Earl; and appeareth in the Form of a Lion, riding upon a Black Horse, and bearing a Viper in his hand. His Office is to discover Things Hidden, Witches, Wizards, and Things Present, Past, and to Come. He, at the command of the Exorcist will build Towers, overthrow Great Stone Walls, and make the Waters rough with Storms. He governeth 36 Legions of Spirits. And his Seal is this, which wear thou, as aforesaid, etc. -Lesser Key of Solomon. Notes: Image created by my art team, sigil from the Lesser Key of Solomon.

**Zagan**

Zagan. He is a Great King and President, appearing at first in the Form of a Bull with Gryphon's Wings; but after a while he putteth on Human Shape. He maketh Men Witty. He can turn Wine into Water, and Blood into Wine, also Water into Wine. He can turn all Metals into Coin of the Dominion that Metal is of. He can even make Fools Wise. He governeth 33 Legions of Spirits, and his Seal is this, etc. - Lesser Key of Solomon. Notes: Image created by my art team, sigil from the Lesser Key of Solomon.

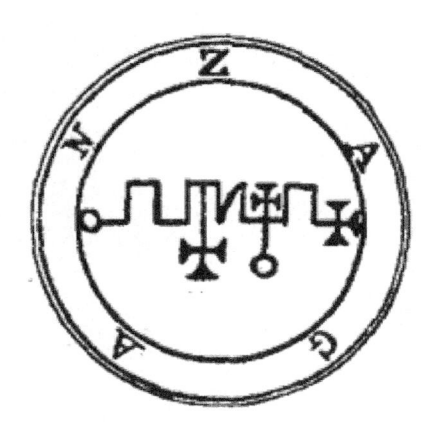

**Zepar**

Zepar. He is a Great Duke, and appeareth in Red Apparel and Armour, like a Soldier. His office is to cause Women to love Men, and to bring them together in love. He also maketh them barren. He governeth 26 Legions of Inferior Spirits, and his Seal is this, which he obeyeth when he seeth it. -Lesser Key of Solomon. Notes: Image created by my art team, sigil from the Lesser Key of Solomon.

# Fairies

**Oberon**

Oberyon a king; he appeareth like a king with a crown on his head. He is under the government of the sun and moon. He teacheth a man knowledge in physic and he showeth the nature of stones, herbs, and trees, and of all metals. He is a great and mighty king, and he is king of the fairies. He causeth a man to be invisible. He showeth where hiding treasure is and how to obtain the same. He telleth of things present, past, and to come, and if he be bound to a man he will bring treasure out of the sea. He holds (or inhabits) the waters and low parts of the earth. -The Book of Oberon. Notes: Sigil by the author.

**Mycob**

Mycob is Queen of the fairies and is of the same office that Oberyon is of. She appeareth in green with a crown on her head and is very meek and gentle. She showeth the nature of herbs, stones, and trees. She showeth the use of medicines and the truth. She causeth the ring of invisibility to be given to the invocator. -The Book of Oberon. Notes: Sigil by the author.

### The 7 sisters

These seven sisters show and teach a man the nature of herbs, and to instruct a man in physic: (health and wellness) also they will bring a man the ring of invisibility. They are under Mycob, the Queen of the fairies. -The Book of Oberon. Notes: Sigils drawn by the author, to match those in the Book of Oberon.

**Lilia**

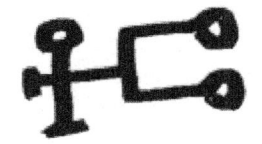

**Rostilia**

**Foca**

**Fola**

# Africa

## Julia

## Venulla

**The Three Sisters**

These three sister fairies are found in the 1584 Discoverie of Witchcraft. They can give the ring of invisibility, and they may also have sex with the magician. They also have the general powers of any other fairies. Sigils created by the author.

**Sibylia**

**Milia**

**Achilia**

**Sibylia, drawn by my art team**

**The Three Queens**

These three Queens (fairies) are found in several old grimoire manuscripts. They give the ring of Invisibility and may also have sex with the magician. They also have the general powers of any other fairies. Sigils created by the author.

**Michel**

**Chicam**

**Burfee**

# The Dead
## Virgil Bird

# Angels

**Michael**

The spirits of the air that belong to Sunday are under the north wind. Their nature is to obtain gold, gems, carbuncles, wealth, favor, and kindness. They dissolve the enmities of men and also grant honor. They can cause or carry away infirmities. Notes: Sigil and text from the Heptameron.

**Gabriel**

The spirits of the air that belong to Monday are beneath the west wind, which is the wind of the moon. Their nature is to give silver, to carry things from place to place, to bestow speed to horses, and to speak secrets both of present and future. Notes: Sigil and text from the Heptameron.

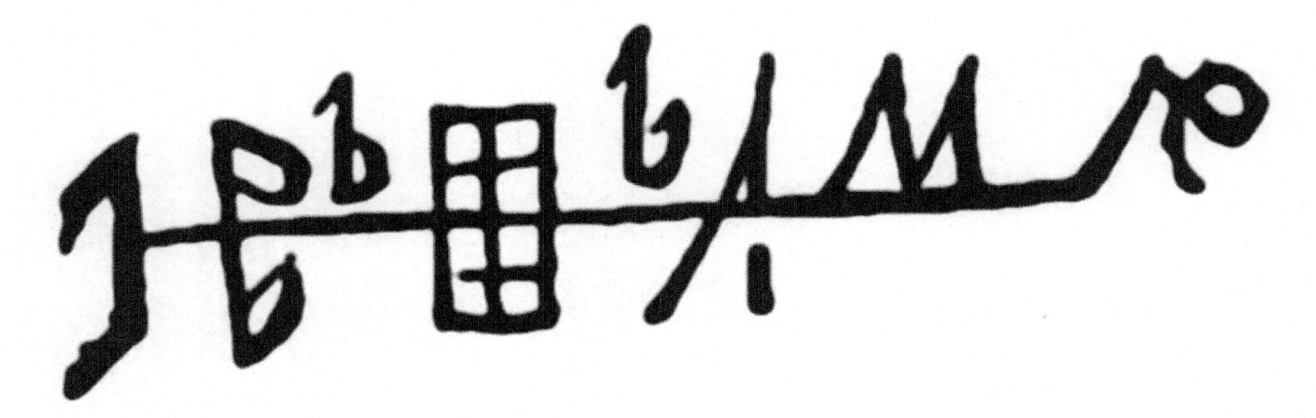

## Samael

The spirits of the air for Tuesday are under the east wind. Their nature is to cause war, death, slayings, and fires. They can bestow 2,000 soldiers at a time. They can give death, infirmity, or health. Notes: Sigil and text from the Heptameron.

## Raphael

The spirits of the air of Wednesday are subject to the southwest wind. Their nature is to give all metals, to reveal all earthly things in the past, the present, and the future. Also to placate judges, and to give victories in war. They teach and re-establish all lost knowledge. They transmute substances from elements that have been mixed, and change conditions from one substance to another. They give sickness or health. They raise the poor and cast down the exalted. They bind spirits or loose their bonds, as well as open locks. Notes: Sigil and text from the Heptameron.

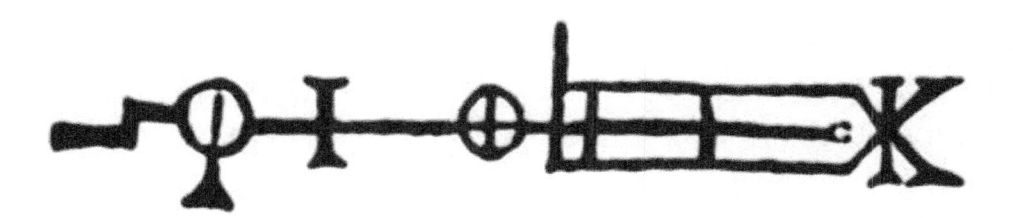

**Sachiel**

The spirits of the air of Thursday are subject to the south wind. Their nature is to win the love of women and to make men joyful and glad of heart. They pacify quarrels and reconcile enemies. They heal the sick and weaken the healthy, and they bring forth or take away injury. Notes: Sigil and text from the Heptameron.

**Anael**

The spirits of the air of Venus (Friday) are subject to the west wind. Their nature is to give silver, to excite men, and to incline them to luxury, and to reconcile enemies through luxury. They make marriages and entice men to love women. They give disease or they can take disease away. They do all things which can bring lust. Notes: Sigil and text from the Heptameron.

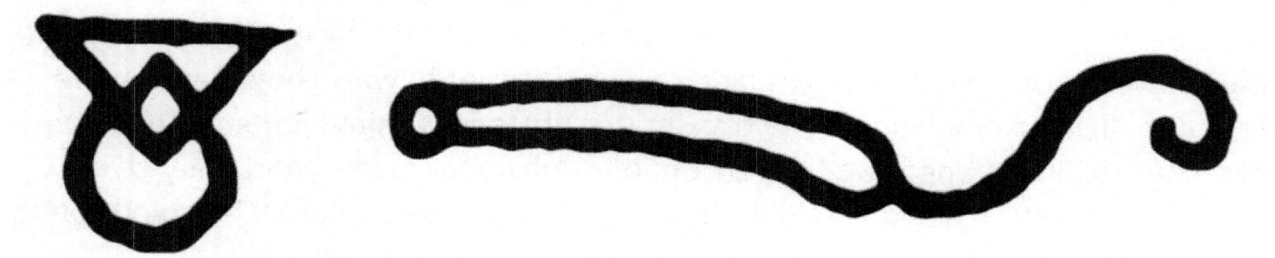

**Cassiel**

The spirits of the air of Saturday are subject to the southwest wind. Their nature is to sow discord, hatred, and evil thoughts. They give lead freely as much as you please. They kill and every member maim. Notes: Sigil and text from the Heptameron.

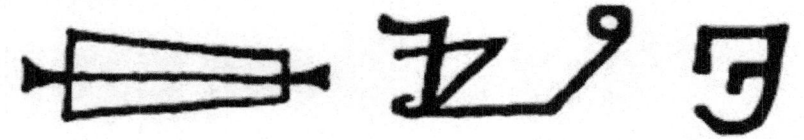

**Metatron**

The angels under Metatron are related to the element of spirit, which rules the other four elements of earth, air, fire, and water. They can give instant awareness of the source of creation, and the form and pattern behind all things. Prima Materia, divine light. Sigil created by the author.

**Notes on the work:**

*Faust conjures Mephistopheles.*

    The Grimoires are the old books of magic. Examples of these books are the Lesser Key of Solomon, Grimorium Verum, Grand Grimoire, Black Dragon, Book of Oberon, Grimoire of Arthur Gauntlet, and others. In the old grimoires, the magician was given methods for conjuring 4 types of spirits. These are: Angels, Demons, Fairies, and the dead. All these spirits were dangerous, even angels, and were conjured while the magician was standing within a magic circle. Most of the time... There are certainly examples of spells where demons are invoked to aid in the spell, and the magician is not standing within a circle. See the spell for nailing an enemy in the Grimorium Verum.

The magician who was brave enough to face the spirits and the inquisition, made a magic circle in secret and raised their wand and conjured the spirits within a magic circle, reading from a book, and usually there was incense burning. These are the basic components of conjuring spirits in the old way. The other component, what I call the key, is a series of body purifications found in all the grimoires. This includes such things as withdrawing from society for a time while moderating the diet, purifying the body, temporary celibacy, long sessions of studying the book or grimoire, and praying to God to forgive you of all your sins. All these things have an effect! **As a general rule, for great power in evocation, go three days celibate (no sex or masturbation) and fast from food the final day.**

During the time the grimoires were written, everyone was a Christian, at least to a degree, even the writers of the grimoires. In our modern age, there is the question of religion and conjuring spirits, because the old grimoires were written within the Christian mythology, and in our age, the world is mixed, and many religions. I am not religious. At his point I have done it all. Yoga, Shamanism, Golden Dawn, traditional grimoires, Demonolatry, etc.

Here is the strange thing about the grimoires. Everything these people were doing was heresy! It did not matter to the Inquisition if a person was conjuring demons by the name of Jesus and the saints. The very fact that they were doing it meant that they were to be executed. The penalty for summoning a demon during the grimoire era was death, no way around that. Even today in some countries you might face severe punishments for getting caught doing the magic in this book.

Yet, the magic of the grimoires was heresy, even if it was written in the Christian framework. The bible clearly condemns Necromancy, the practice of conjuring the dead. And Fairies are a pagan creature. There are no fairies in the bible. And even the demons themselves such as Astaroth, Beelzebub, and Leviathan can be traced back to pagan gods along with many others. There is strong evidence that the angels were borrowed from Zoroastrianism, which was in turn built from early Iranian polytheism. Yahweh once had a wife. It's all very complex. Asherah, Elohim, Semitic Pantheon. Etc.

I could easily write several hundred more pages here on magic circles, various grimoires, and the origin of spirits. But my purpose here is to provide a book that is to be used to call spirits, and not explain them. For that, see my other 30 books. And you know the religious structure of the west. The Bible, Heaven, and Hell, all of that. What I really want to say here is that if you build a magic circle, and get a wand and some incense, open this book up and start trying to conjure the spirits, wonderful things will happen.

I do not believe that the spirits are all good or all evil. If you look at the powers of the angels described in this book, they are the same as the demons. They were all pagan gods before Christianity came along, and to me they are all pagan gods once again, or simply spirits. They all have their own personalities, and desires, and magic. Its all magic. This method is Universal. It is simply a series of steps to conjure a spirit and send it back. The bornless one is God, and God is a power, an energy.

I am a universalist. I am all religions; I am no religion. I am a spiritual scientist. The Bornless one is not any one god or goddess, it's the force beyond duality, the Tao. The Bornless one is not El, not Yahweh, not Asherah, not the Elohim, it's above all that, closer to electricity.

At your core, you are a spark of the great flame, and the Bornless one is the great flame. All other gods move within the great flame, its all one vast field of energy. Everything is energy. The more energy you can store within your body the easier it will be to see and interact with all these creatures. Angels, Demons, Fairies, and the dead.

It should be noted that there is another way to do all of this. You can do it without a circle and wand, look at the candles burned all over the world for saints and angels and demons and the dead. Either way you will reach out and make a connection. And sometimes you will use one way and sometimes you will use another.

The wand is like a radio antenna it picks up and receives vibrations from the universe. Beyond this I need say no more, you will learn the rest from the spirits. This book is a universal way of encountering a spirit, then sending it away, back to its home. It can still come back later. Its ok, you're not torturing or binding the spirit, just calling it. Be respectful with the method, and you will do fine. Keep your tools put away when not in use, to keep the area in a stable rate of vibration.

Concerning the dead... There is only one ghost here in this book and his name is Virgil Bird. Virgil was a good friend of mine and I have a right to conjure him. You will have to find your own ghosts, or you may try to conjure Virgil Bird. He said it was ok. He knew he was going to be in this book he saw it all in visions. He told me all this telepathically. I don't care if you believe me on any of that. Conjuring ghosts is a bit different than conjuring other spirits.

One last thing to say, Energy. How much energy you have is how much you're going to see spirits. This comes in many forms. That's why the grimoires were always raving about not having sex before conjuring. Because going without sex bottles up the energy. Also, your diet, your procedure. Clean your room. Clean your body. The Goetia talks about working on the Waxing moon, a time of greater energy. The magic circle is like a spaceship to other worlds. You are moving yet standing still.

If you want to study all this more, I go into detail in my book Fairy Magic in the Grimoires, and Sibylia: Fairy Magic in the 1584 Discovery of Witchcraft. My book Magic circles shows at least 50 variations of the magic circle from old grimoires. I have released editions of the Lesser Key, Grand Grimoire, Grimorium Verum, Black Dragon, and Grimoire of Pope Honorius, etc. I also teach how to get incredible amounts of energy in my book UEF, how to leave the body and perform astral projection in my book Flying Lessons, and general sorcery strategy and how to move in the world in my book The Sorcery Party.

All these books are valuable areas of study to be a complete witch or sorcerer. For that is what you hold in your hands, a book of sorcery. I could rant and rave about what seeing the spirits is like, but I have done that in my book the Lore of Asmoday and Illustrated Goetia. And if you want to learn the history behind all of this, you will enjoy the Legend of Astaroth, etc. I have written a lot of Books! Those were my adventures. Now it is time to make your own memories. I wish you the best of luck on the path.

-Arundell Overman

## Creation of the Universal Conjuring Circle

Universal conjuring circle, lesson 1

Hello friends, here I am teaching a 4-part lesson on how to create the universal conjuring circle. This is a circle I designed, and I hope that you can pick up some tips for your own work. Making magic circles is an art that must be adapted based on the size and complexity of the work.

The first thing to do is to determine the center of the circle. In this case, my carpet is 4 ft 6 in by 6 ft 6 in. I know I want a little extra room on the edge of the circle, so how much should that be? After carefully measuring the carpet, I determine that a circle that is 4 ft across would leave 3 inches of extra room on each side. Therefore, to get my center point of the circle, it needs to be 2 ft, plus three inches up from the bottom of the carpet.

I start by dividing the carpet in half, and then measure upwards on the center line to a distance of 27 inches, this gives me my 2 feet (which is half of the distance across the circle) PLUS the 3 inches on the edge of the circle. Thus, I can calculate the center point of the circle by measuring 27 inches upwards from the bottom, on that imaginary center line of the carpet. Once I find that important point, I can use a ruler to measure from the center outward, 2 feet, and then make a tiny dot. Doing this over and over makes a circle of dots, and I can connect those dots to make the circle. This gives us our basic circle, in place, and we will move to more complex parts in the next lesson.

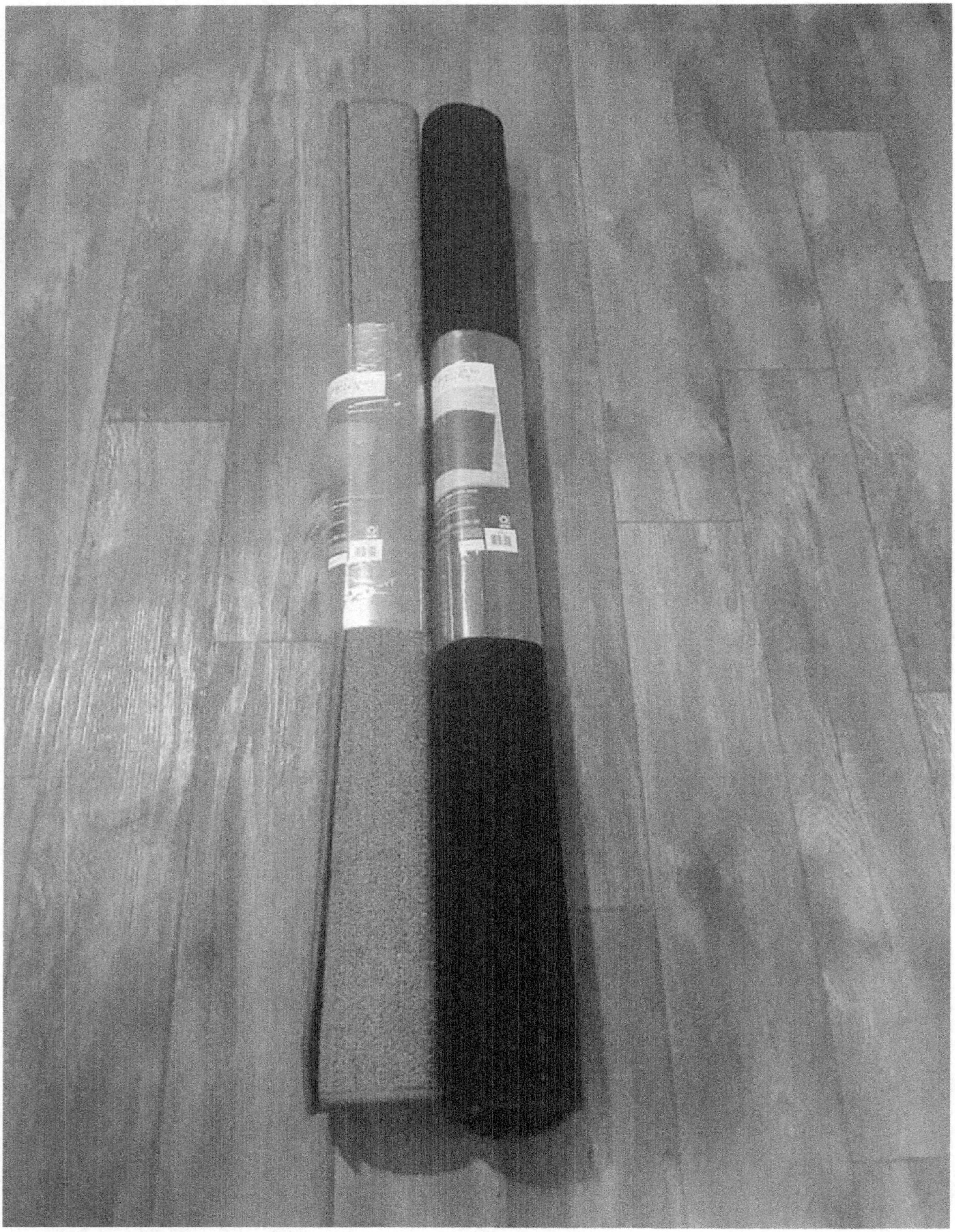

Titan Pecan
4ft 6in x 6ft 6in
Area Rug
-traffic areas
sold separately)
cm x 198.1 cm)
Titan Black
4ft 6in x 6ft 6in
Area Rug
Tapete de área color negro
titán de 1.3 x 1.9 m
Durable for high-traffic areas
Durable para áreas muy transitadas
Stain resistant
Rug pad recommended (sold separately)
54 in x 78 in (137.1 cm x 198.1 cm)

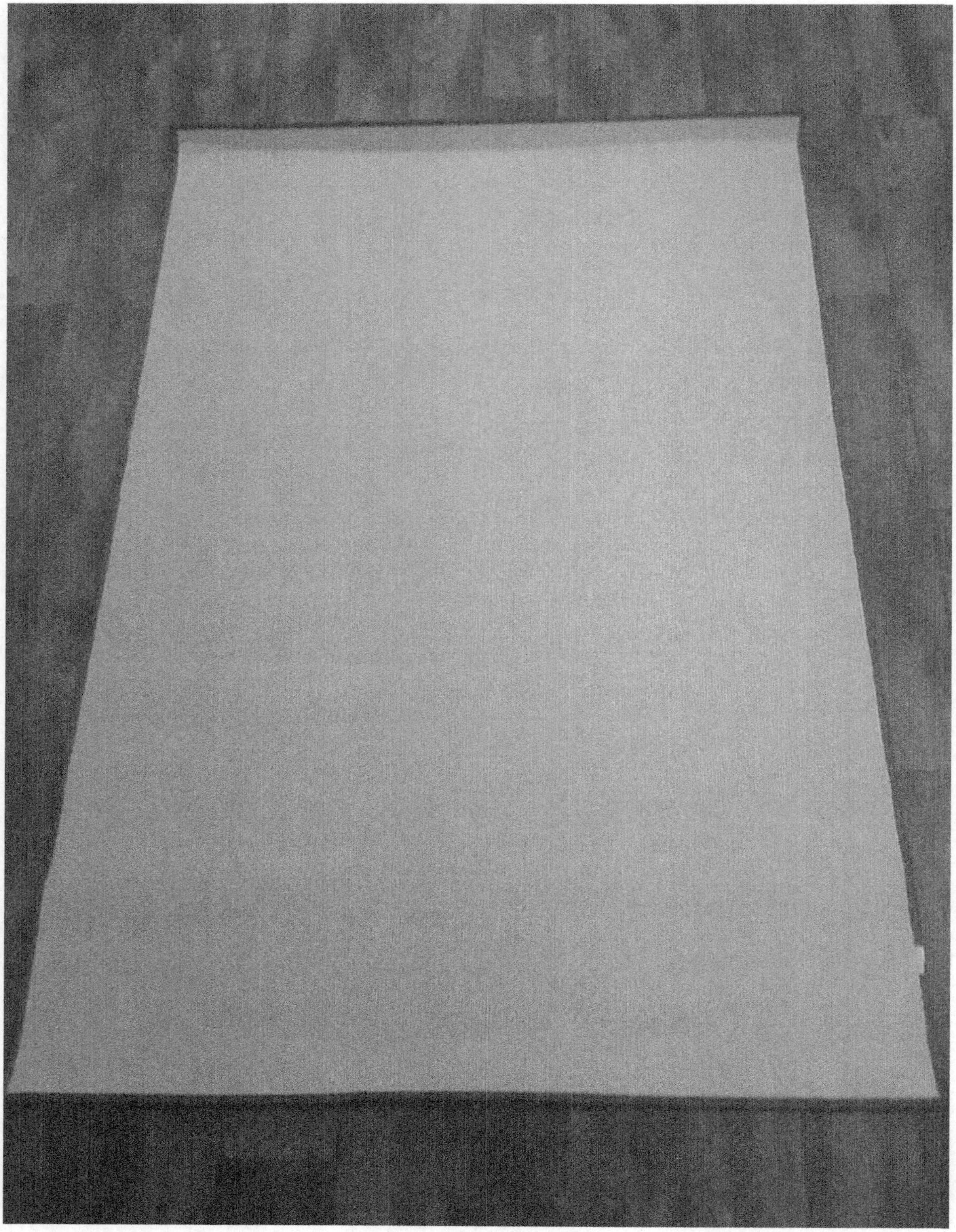

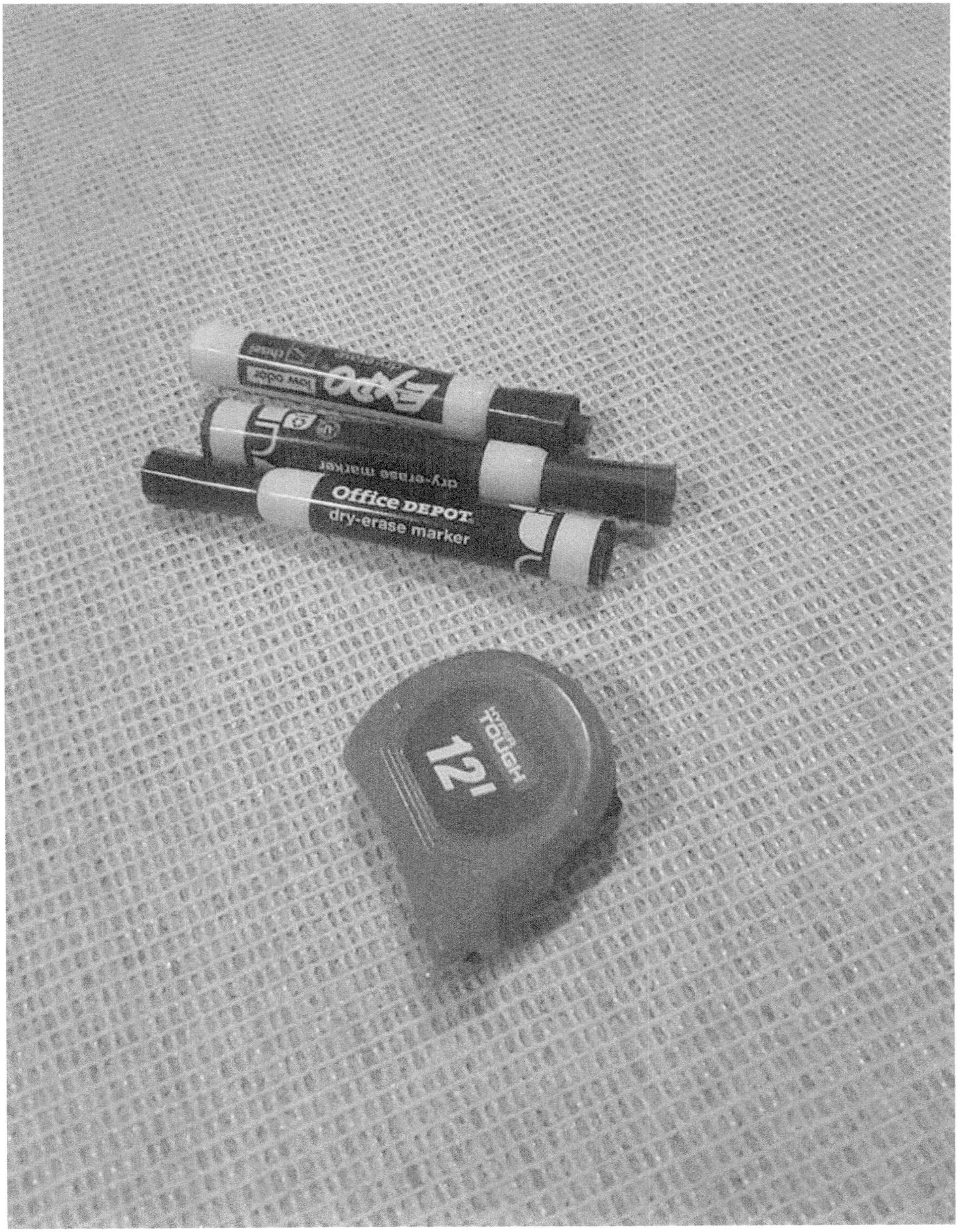
Office DEPOT
dry-erase marker
12'

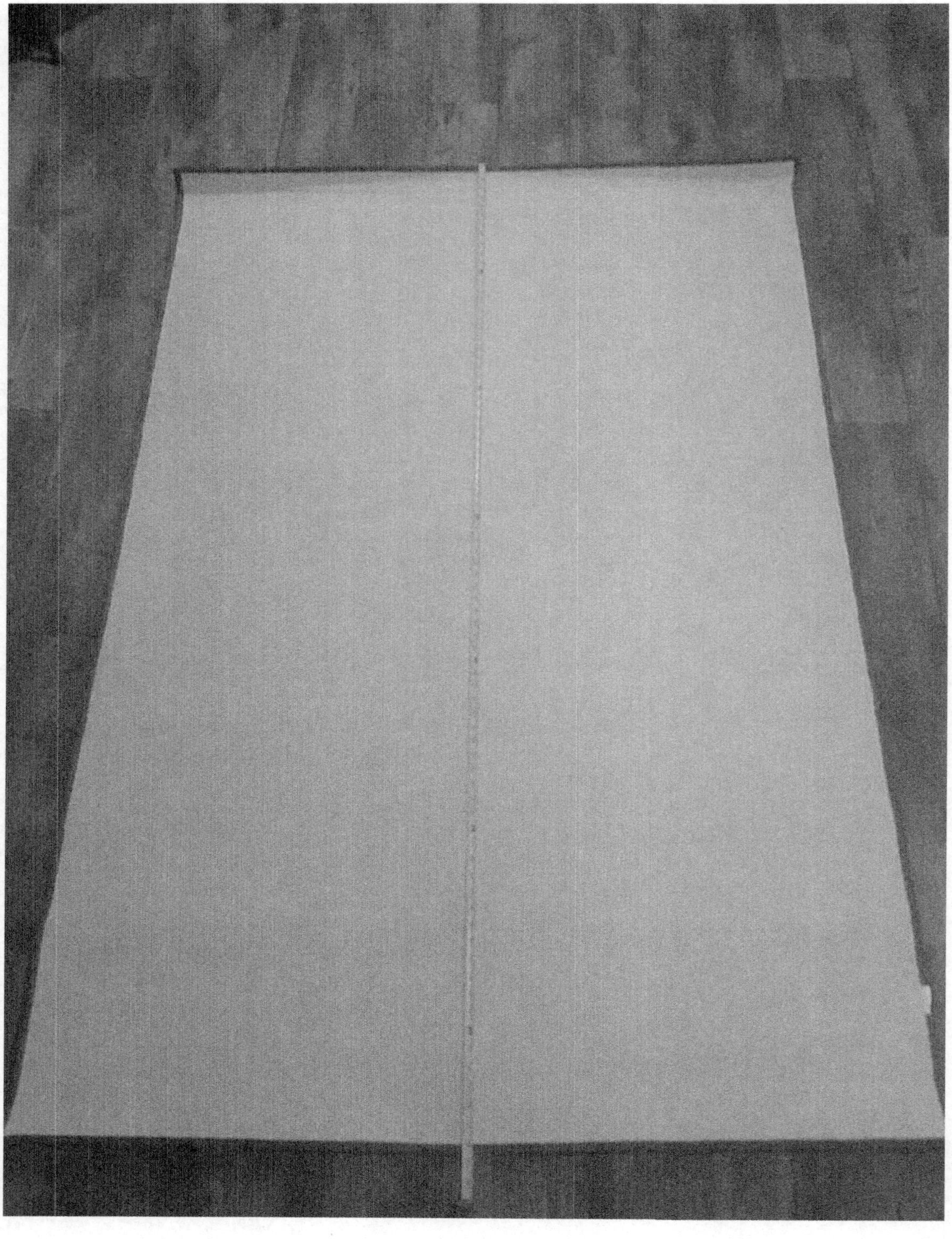

> Size of carpet is 4 ft 6 in by 6 ft 6 in. Circle is 4 ft across with three inches at the edge. Center point is 27 in from the bottom of the carpet.
>
> 2 ft
>
> 3 in →

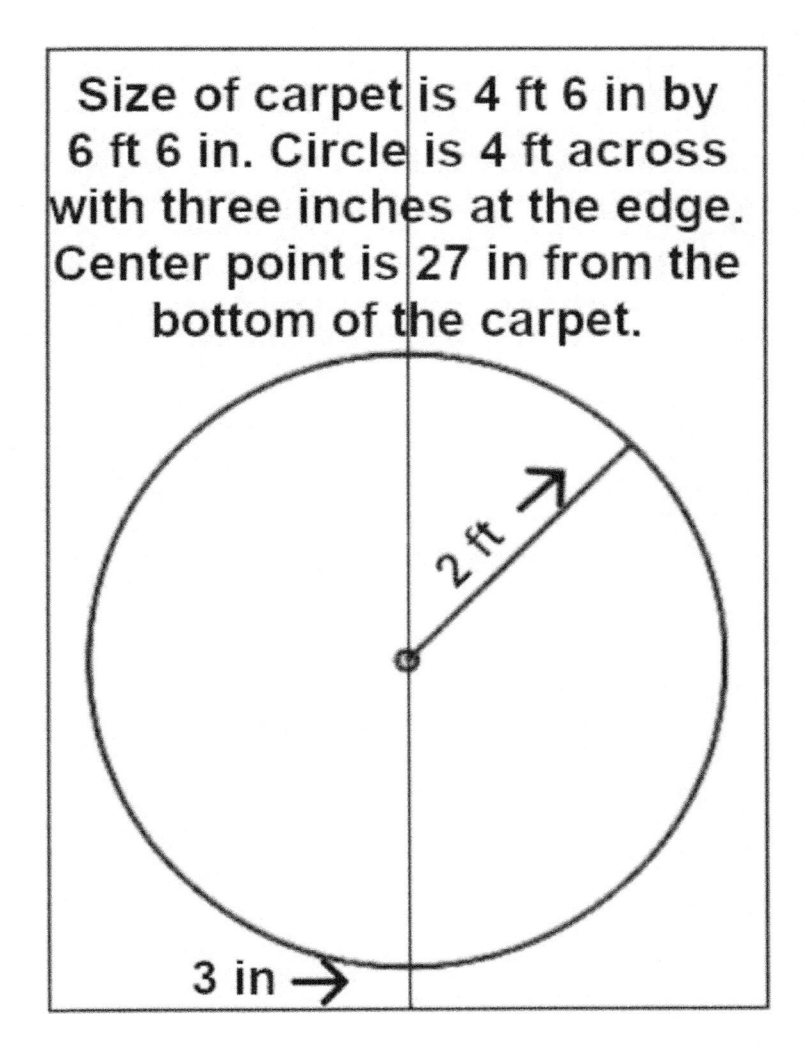

Circle making class, lesson 2

Ok, so what I am showing here is the center of the circle, and how it can be "double checked" with the outer edges so you can begin drawing on the dots. With this method, now that I have double (and sometimes triple) checked everything, you will place the ruler or measuring stick at the center and make a dot with your marker at the edge of what will be your circle. In this case, my circle is 4 ft across, so from the center of the circle to the edge is 2 ft.

Now, since this circle is going to have two bands on the inside, I want to go ahead and make a mark on my ruler at 1 ft 6 inches for my first band, and one ft for my second band. That way, as I am making the outer circle, I can make the dots for the inner bands as well, this saves time, and you don't have to go around the circle three times. In the picture shown below, you can see a plexiglass box, that's my altar, and I am using it as my ruler as well. I take the measuring tape, and measure the exact places on the plexiglass box, (make a dot there on the box itself with the marker) and then, by touching its bottom edge to the center of the circle and making my marks. I then move it forward a few inches and make another few marks. And so on. If the center of the circle point is in the right place, everything else will be as well. When all the dots are made, all the way around the circle, simply connect the dots, and you have your basic outline of the circle.

It should be 27 inches from the center of the circle to the edge of the carpet. The line extends out from the center by 2 ft. Circle=4 ft across.

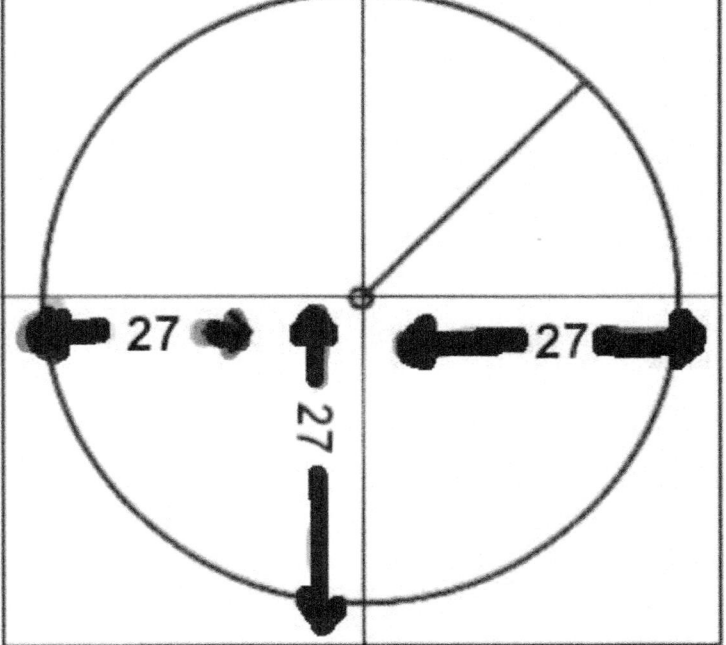

27   27

27

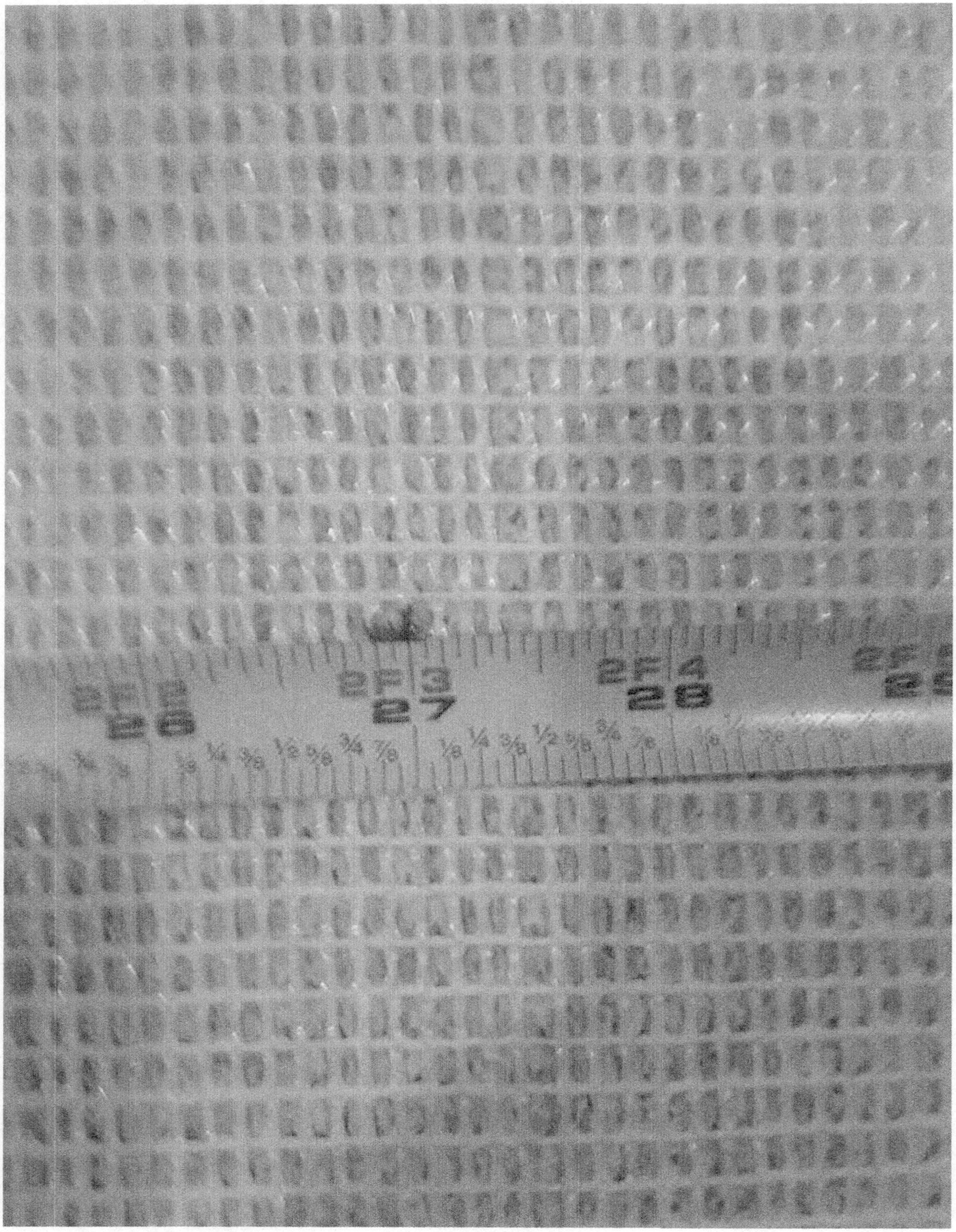
2F3
27
2F4
28

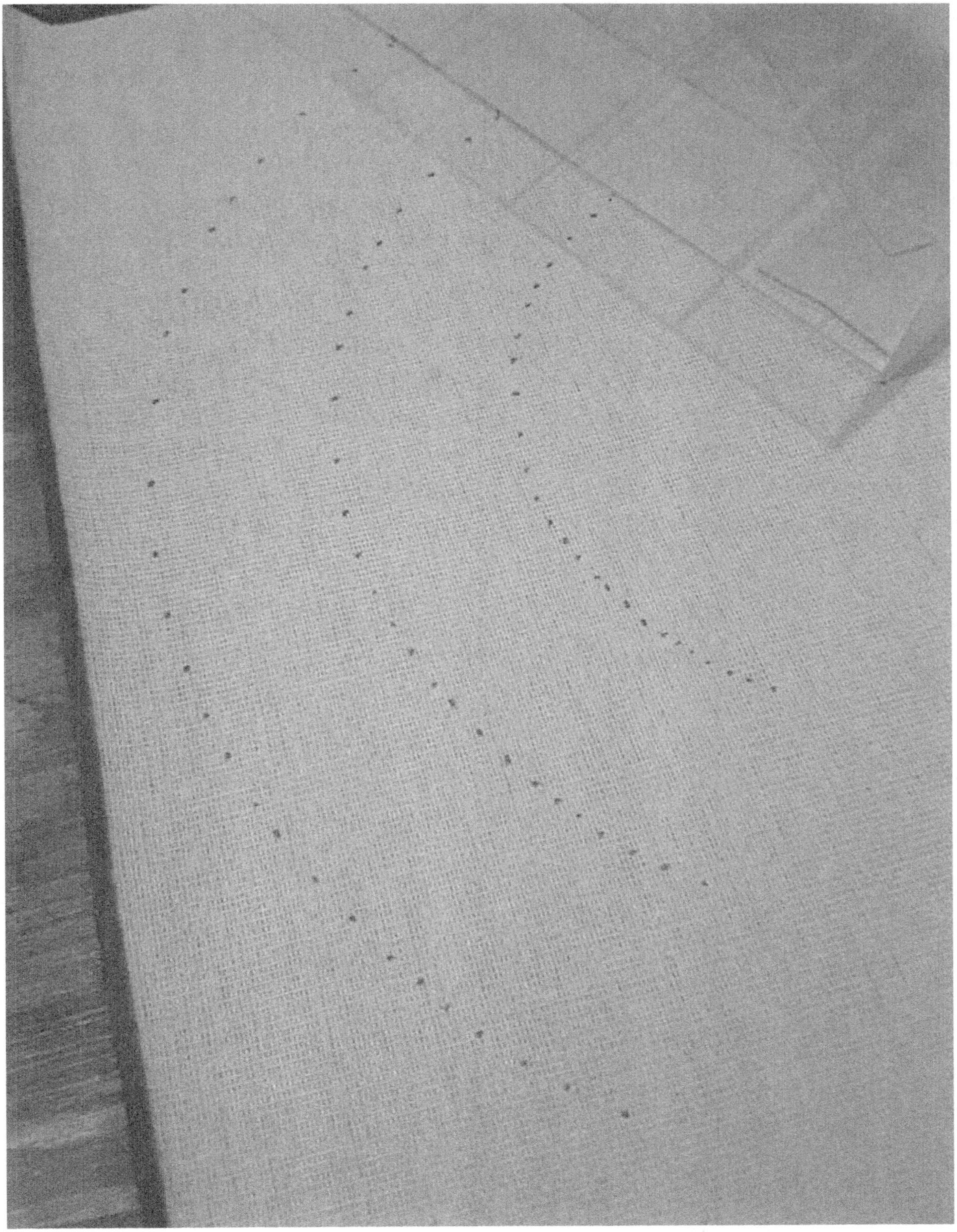

Circle creation class, lesson 3

Ok, so continuing with showing how I created this circle. Once you have your center point established, you begin to make a series of dots with your marker. The design of this circle calls for 2 inner bands, so, to make the outer edge of the circle and both bands at once, I decided that the thickness of each band would be 6 inches.

So, touching the tip of my ruler to the center, I made a dot at 2 ft, and then came inward towards the center by 6 in and made another dot, then came inward another 6 inches and made another dot. This process is slow, and it can take at least 15 or 20 minutes to go around the whole circle, but it sets you up for smooth, nicely drawn lines. Once all your dots are created, simply connect them and you will have your basic form of the circle.

Touch the end of your ruler to the center, make a mark at 2 ft, 1 ft 6 in, and one ft, to make each band 6 in thick. Do this many times then connect the dots.

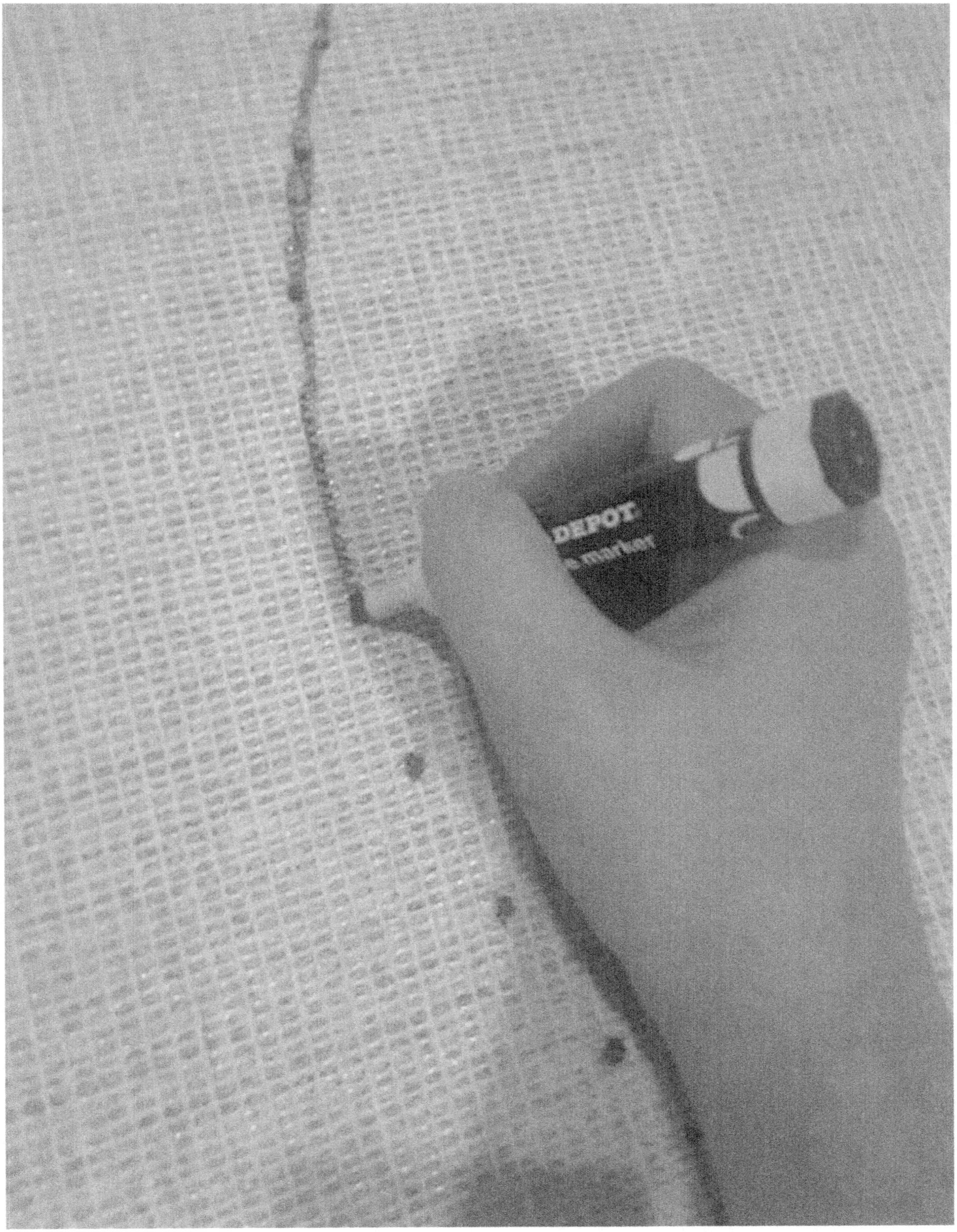
DEPOT

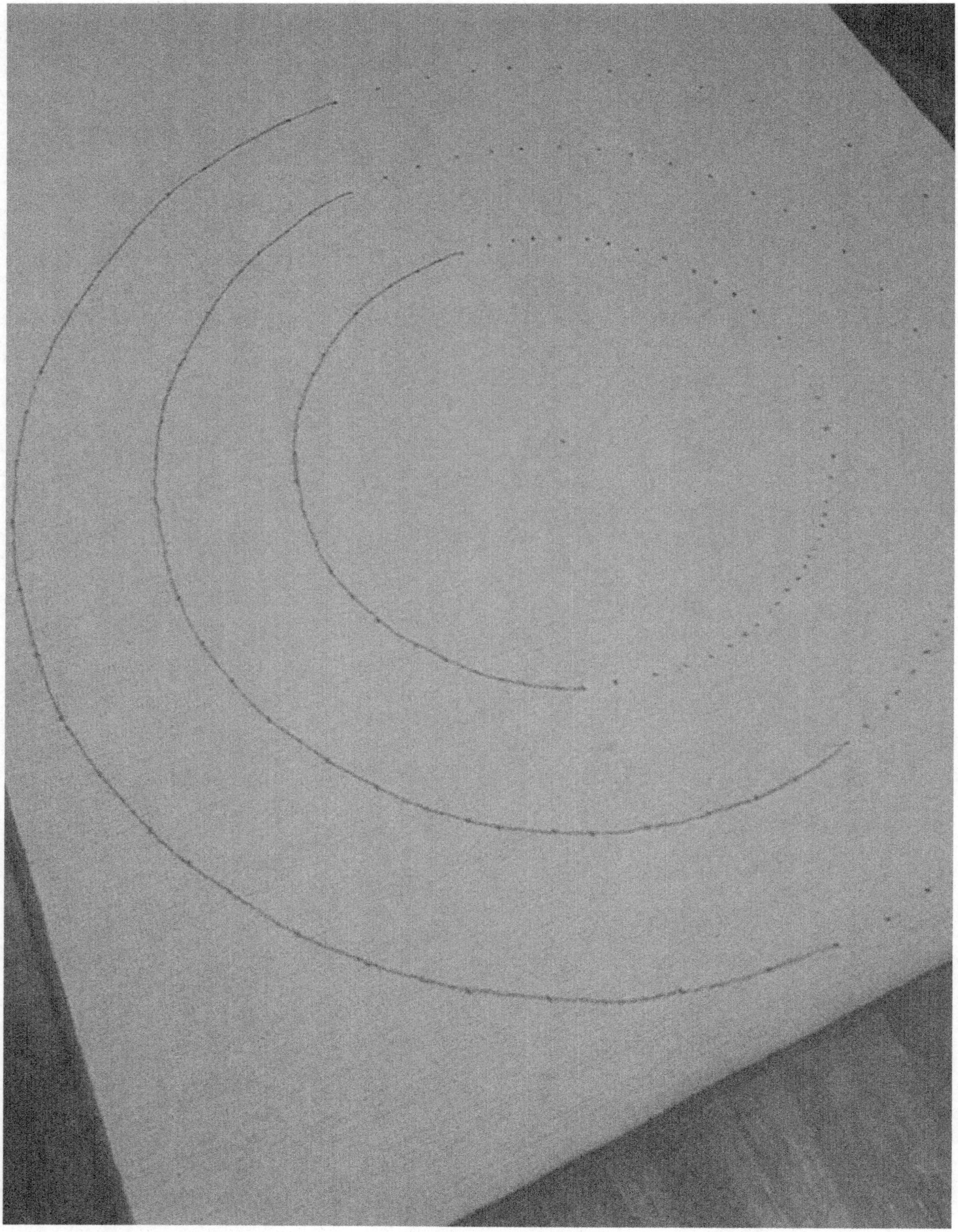

Circle creation class, lesson 4

Ok, so you can see that, at this stage, I connect all the dots I made in the previous lessons, and the first outline of the circle takes shape. Now to place the triangle where the spirits will appear. This is a bit tricky, but I have several clues as to where this should go. First, I know that I want the tip of the triangle to be placed on the imaginary center line, this will keep it center.

And I also know that the base of the triangle should be level with the top of the carpet. So, what I decided was, let's bring the tip if the triangle inward, on that imaginary line by 3 inches. This gives me a definite spot that the tip of the triangle will touch, so I make a make a dot there. Then, I know that I would like for the base of the triangle to be about three inches away from the circle. So, I make a dot on the imaginary center line, up three inches from the edges of the circle.

Then, I lay my ruler down on that base of the triangle line, (check it with the top of the carpet) and draw outward 6 inches each way. This gives me a good base line to work with. In this instance, I am making a triangle that has equal sides, so I will measure the base, and then check the sides, then measure the base, draw the line a little longer, and check the sides. After a few times of doing this, the triangle begins to form, and I can use my ruler to make neat even lines. The lines are thin at this point, because I am just putting on basic shapes, and at the end, will go over every design again to deepen the lines.

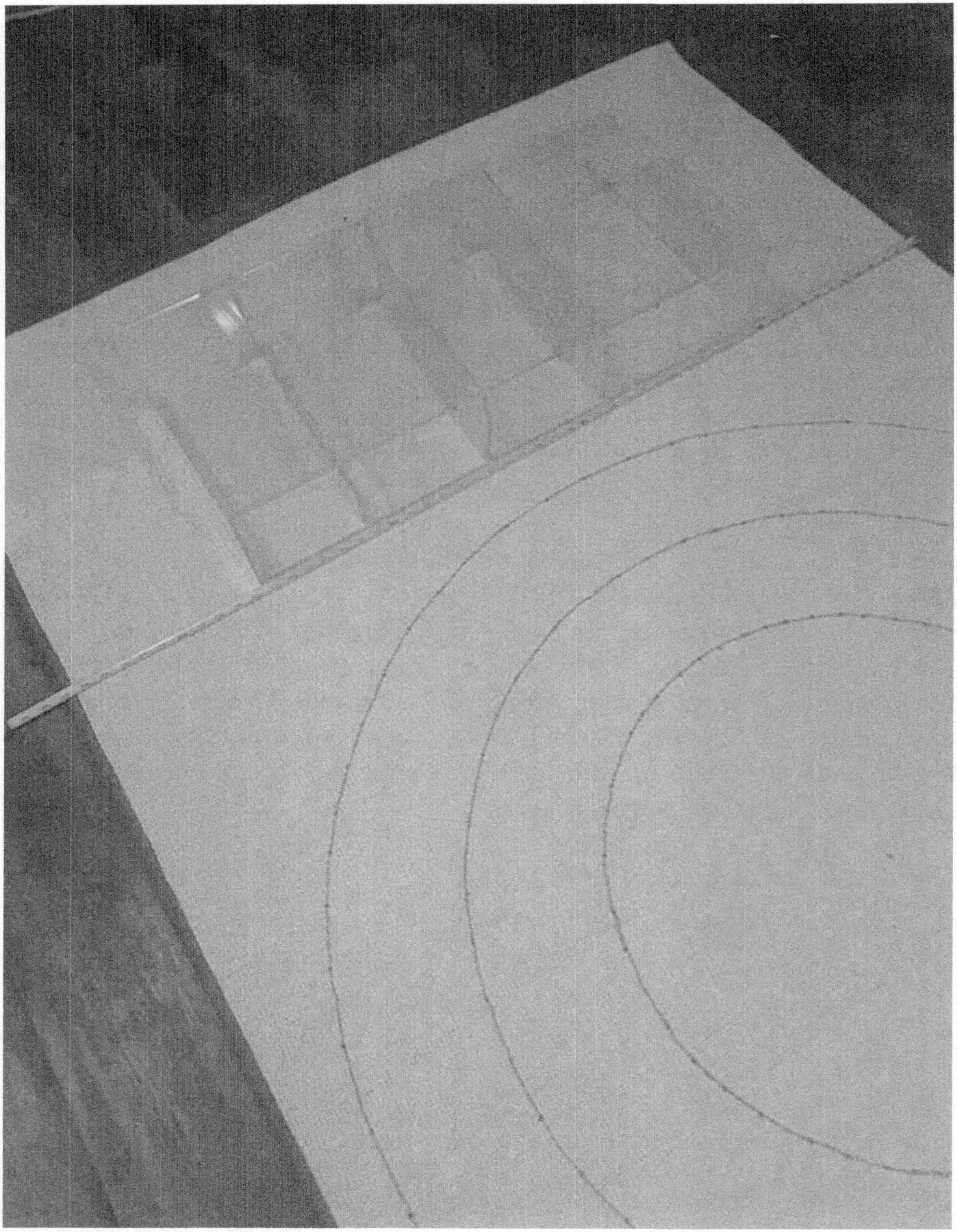

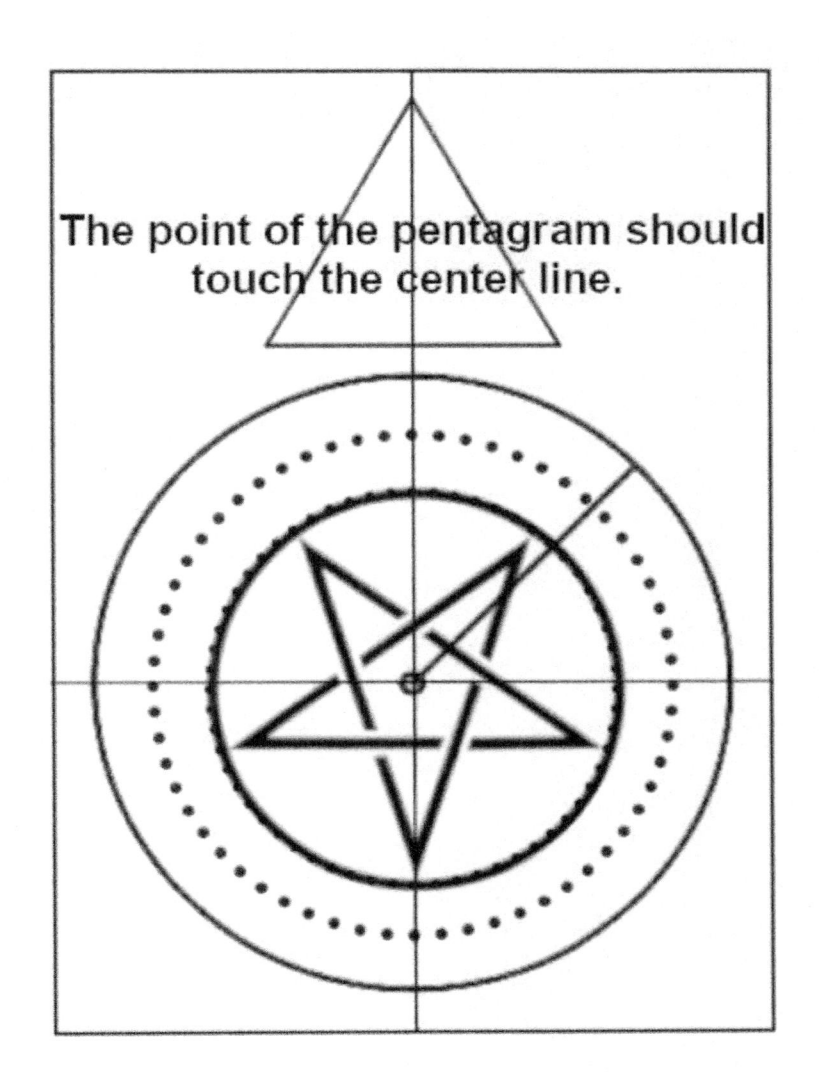

The point of the pentagram should touch the center line.

216 | Page

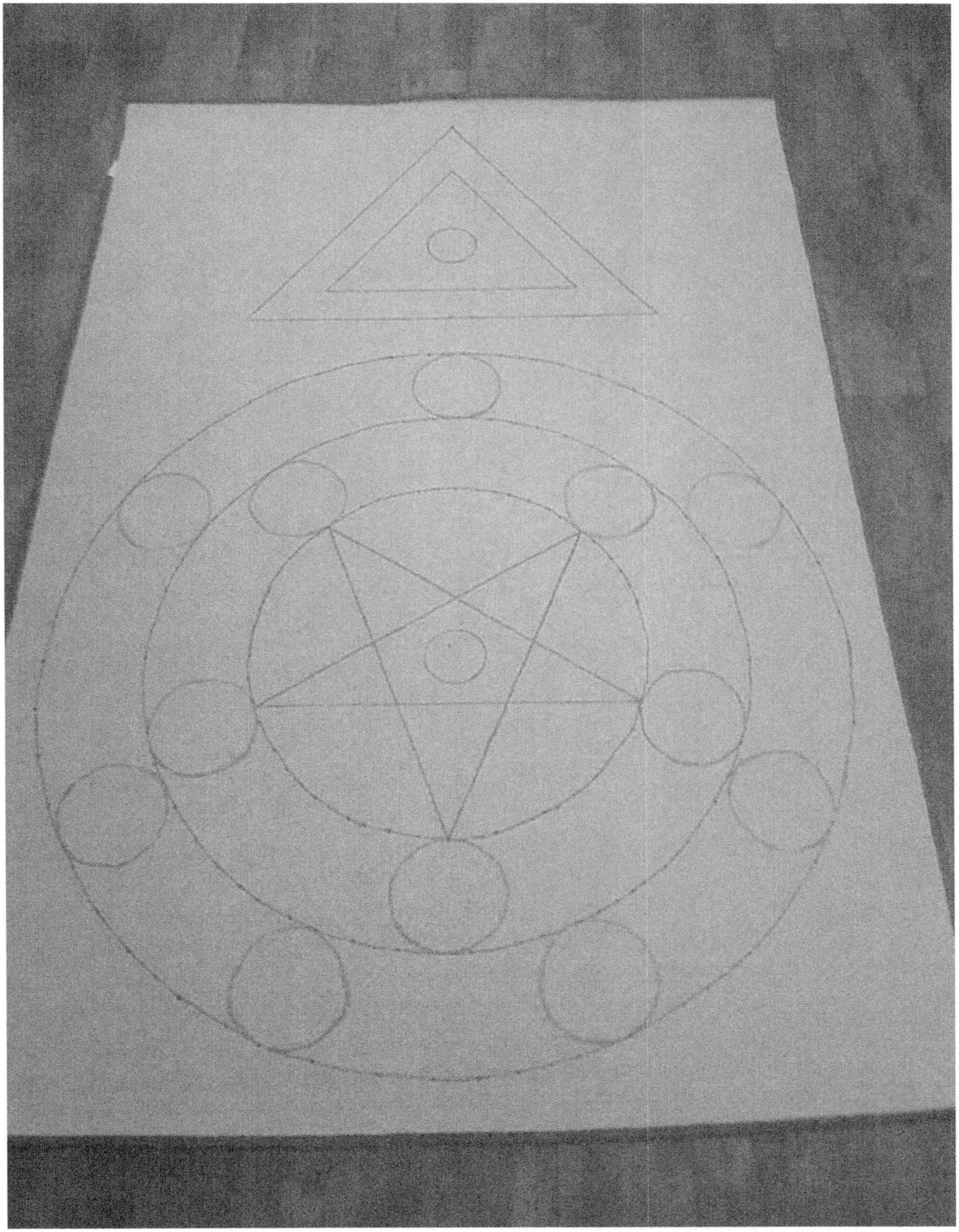

218 | Page

A line from the center to the corner will show you where to place the stars. Make sure the tip of each is at an equal distance from the edge of the circle.

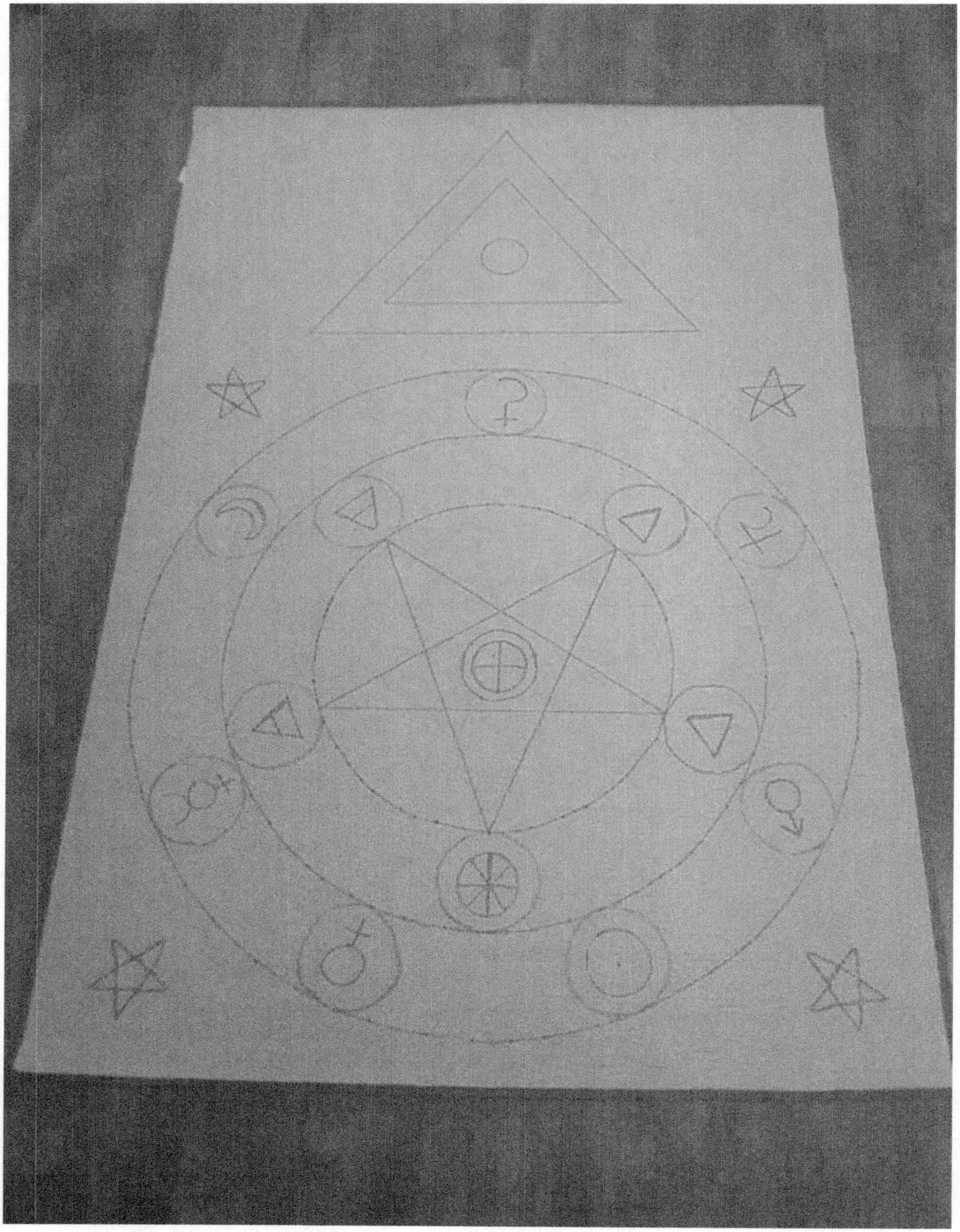

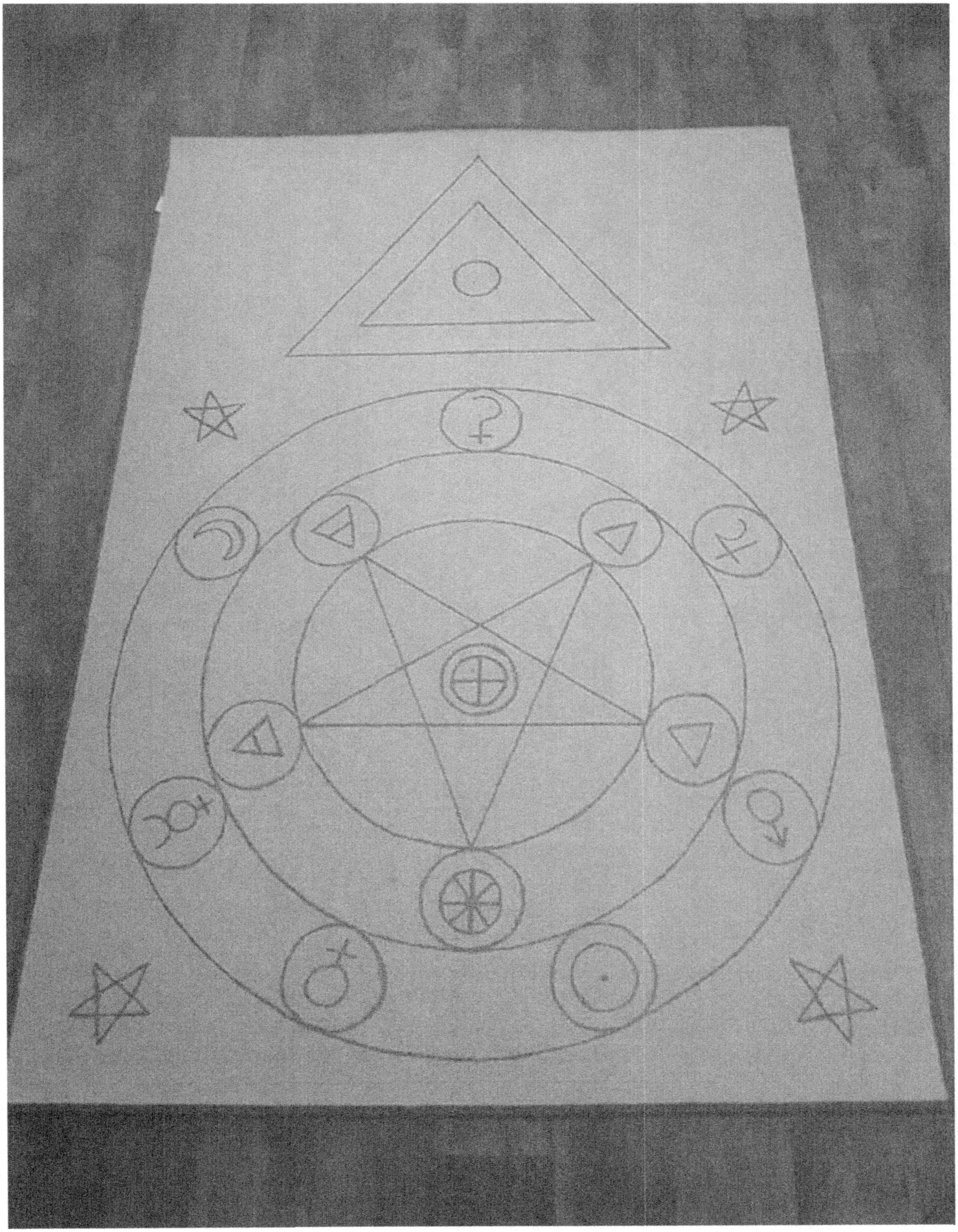

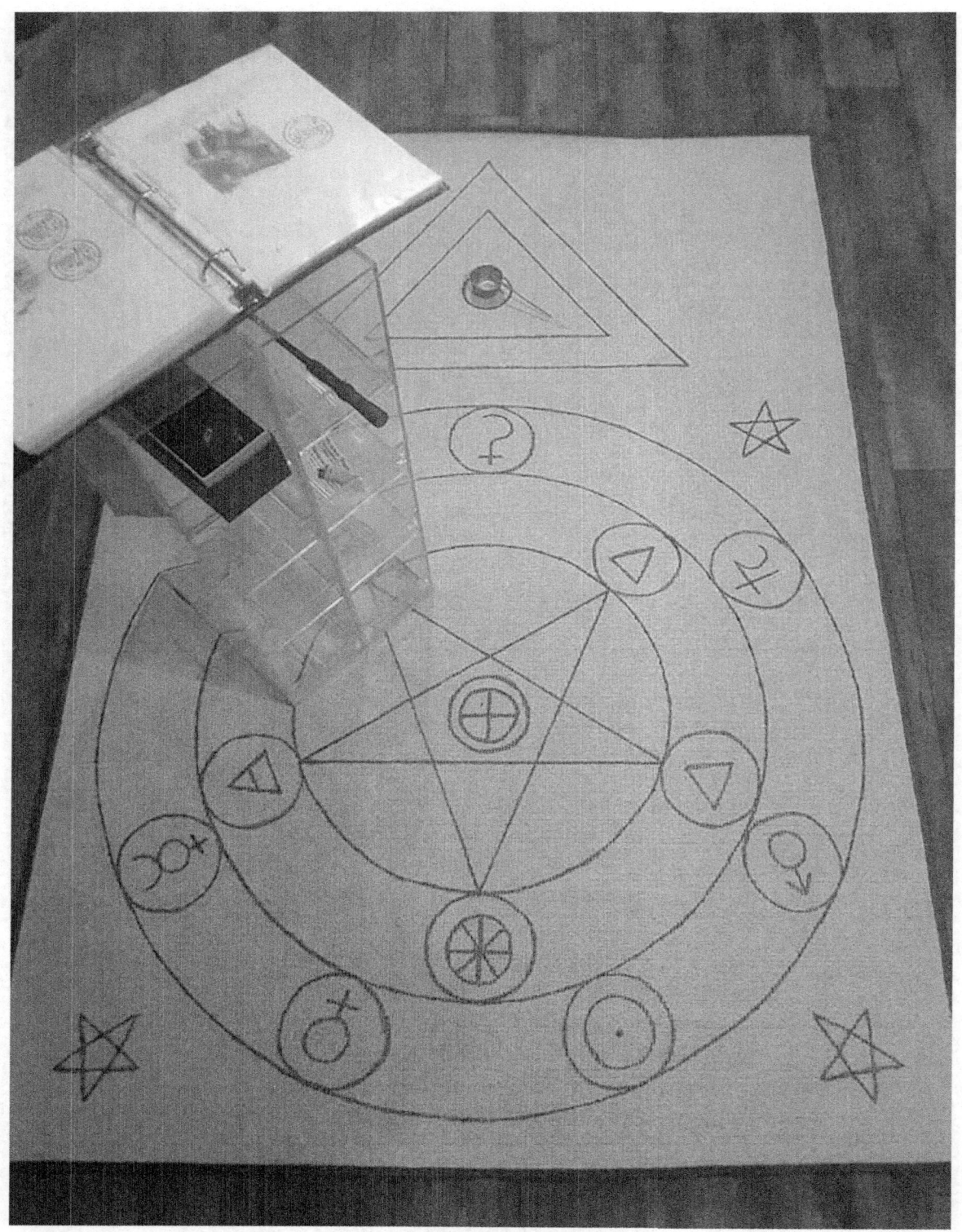

All set up to conjure spirits

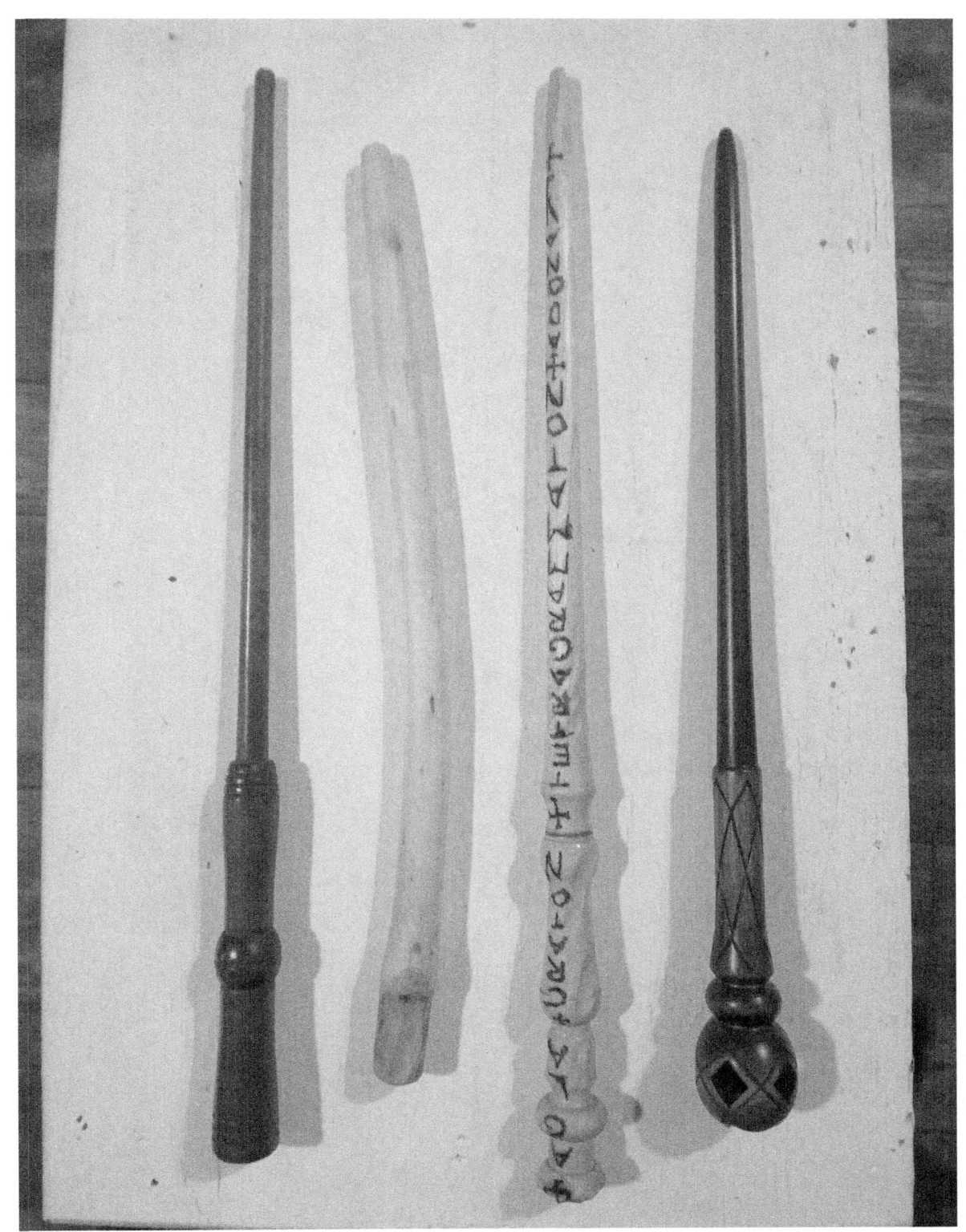

Magic Wands

Incense

Notes:

Notes:

Back CVR: The Grimoire of Arundell is an instruction manual for conjuring a vast array of spirits. One method is given to conjure Angels, Demons, Fairies, and the Dead. Also included are step by step instructions on how to create and use a magic circle. Spirits include the demons Agaliarept, Agares, Aglasis, Aim, Alloces, Amdusias, Amy, Andras, Andrealphus, Andromalius, Amon, Asmodeus, Astaroth, Azazel, Bael, Balam, Barbatos, Bathin, Bechard, Beleth, Belial, Belzebub, Berith, Bifrons, Botis, Brulefer, Bucon, Buer, Bune, Camio, Cemejes, Claunech, Clisthert, Crocell, Dantalion, Decarabia, Egyn, Elelogap, Eligos, Fleurety, Focalor, Foras, Forneus, Frimost, Frucissiere, Frutimiere, Furcas, Furfur, Gaap, Glasya-Labolas, Gremory, Guland, Gusion, Haagenti, Hael, Halphus, Haristum, Haures, Heramael, Hicpacth, Huictigaras, Humots, Ipos, Khil, Klepoth, Leraje, Leviathan, Lilith, Lucifer, Lucifuge, Rofocale, Malphas, Marax, Marbas, Marchosias, Mersilde, Minoson, Morail, Murmur, Musisin, Naberius, Nebiros, Oriax, Oriens, Orobas, Ose, Paimon, Pentagnony, Phenex, Proculo, Pruflas, Purson, Raum, Ronove, Sabnock, Sallos, Samigina, Sargatanas, Satanachia, Scirlin, Seere, Segal, Sergulath, Serguthy, Shax, Sidragosam, Sirchade, Sitri, Stolas, Surgat, Sustugriel, Syrach, Trimasael, Uvall, Valak, Valefor, Vapula, Vassago, Vepar, Vine, Zagan, and Zepar. The Fairies Oberon, Mycob, Lilia, Rostilia, Foca, Fola, Africa, Julia, Venulla, Sibylia, Milia, Achilia, Michel, Chicam, and Burfee. The Dead, V.B. And the angels Michael, Gabriel, Samael, Raphael, Sachiel, Anael, Cassiel, and Metatron.

Printed in Great Britain
by Amazon